# Take Your Glory Lord

## Mary Garnett

Sovereign World

Sovereign World Ltd
PO Box 777
Tonbridge
Kent TN11 0ZS
England

ISBN 1 85240 254 7

This Sovereign World book is distributed in North America by Renew
Books, a ministry of Gospel Light, Ventura, California, USA. For a free
catalog of resources from Renew Books/Gospel Light, please contact
your Christian supplier or call 1-800-4-GOSPEL.

Typeset by CRB Associates, Reepham, Norfolk.
Printed in England by Clays Ltd, St Ives plc.

# Contents

| | *Foreword to the Original Edition* | 5 |
|---|---|---|
| | *Preface by Peter Lyne* | 8 |
| *Chapter 1* | The Herd Boy | 11 |
| *Chapter 2* | The Call of God! | 19 |
| *Chapter 3* | Surrounded by Glory | 24 |
| *Chapter 4* | A Church of Prayer | 32 |
| *Chapter 5* | Pastor Duma | 40 |
| *Chapter 6* | A Blaze of Glory | 49 |
| *Chapter 7* | New Horizons | 54 |
| *Chapter 8* | The Power of Discerning Prayer | 63 |
| *Chapter 9* | Three Women Are Healed | 69 |
| *Chapter 10* | Changed Lives | 78 |
| *Chapter 11* | Prisoners of Christ | 88 |
| *Chapter 12* | Making Friends with Worldly Wealth | 99 |

| | | |
|---|---|---|
| *Chapter 13* | The Witchdoctor | 108 |
| *Chapter 14* | A Healer Healed | 112 |
| *Chapter 15* | William Duma and His Boys | 119 |
| *Chapter 16* | No Other Name | 126 |
| *Chapter 17* | A Man for All Seasons, A Man for All Places, A Man for All Races | 133 |
| | A Brief Tribute | 139 |
| | Key to Zulu words | 140 |

# Foreword

I first read *Take Your Glory Lord* some weeks before I had reason to visit South Africa on business. The book left such a deep impression that I made a point of locating the author in Durban, where she lived with her companion Ninna Larsen.

Mary Garnett (*nom de plum* of the author Joan Goddard) had spent many years on mission stations with her father, a Congregational minister, before settling in Durban, where she worked for the Health Department, primarily concerned with the health needs of Zulu women.

During her work, she came to hear of the healing ministry of a Zulu Baptist minister at the Umgeni Road Baptist Church, a corrugated iron structure set beside a hotel in a low income area of Durban. The way some people put Duma on a pedestal tended to upset her, and she refused to go anywhere near him. However, the time came when she was advised by her Department to get Duma's support in promoting more hygienic baby feeding methods among the Zulu women.

She said, 'He seemed such a humble little man and immediately agreed to help me by involving all his church women in the programme. As I was about to leave the church, I turned to him and said, "Pastor, I want to warn you, there have been many cases of famous evangelists falling by the wayside, letting the adulation of the crowds turn their heads.'' '

Duma looked at her through his glasses and said, 'Oh yes, Miss Goddard, I am very conscious of that. Every time I stand to speak in the pulpit I look up to my Lord and say under my breath, "Take Your glory, Lord. Take Your glory." '

Joan and Ninna recounted the growing relationship that developed between Joan's father and Duma after their initial meeting. Subsequent to Reverend Goddard's death, Joan continued meeting with Duma, often helping him construct a talk in better English than his grasp of the language allowed, on those occasions when he needed to speak to non-Zulus.

Eventually, she was led to write his story, a work completed only a short time before he died in Durban in 1979; and she granted the Baptist Missionary Society rights to publish the book in South Africa, where it has subsequently passed through at least seven reprints (as last reported in 1985).

As she completed each chapter, invariably after many weeks of sifting through his taped recollections, he would come and listen to her read the manuscript. At times he would nod again and again as a story retold touched him with a special reality; occasionally, tears would trickle down his furrowed cheeks and he would say, 'Oh, that is it, that is it! You have made it come alive. That is how it was.' As he viewed his life and work, it is not surprising that he gave no thought to records or diaries, still less to future biography. The stories related in this chronicle are not, therefore, always in order of time.

Joan Goddard's prime concern was that the works of Duma be shared as widely as possible, as any who have read the book will appreciate. In the midst of contemporary Christian literature, *Take Your Glory Lord* will in time, take its place alongside such life changing publications as David Wilkerson's *The Cross and the Switchblade* and Basilea

Schlink's *Realities*, and others of like stature. Of that, I am sure the reader will agree.

### *Keith N. Cleland PhD, FCPA*
Consultant to Industry and the Accounting Profession,
previously Professor of Accounting,
Co-Founder International Christian
Chamber of Commerce.

**Publisher's Note**
*Take Your Glory Lord* was written at a time when apartheid was taken for granted as a way of life, and as such does not presume to challenge this regime. In fact, the grace and dignity which the black Christians in this book maintain whilst living under such oppression is one of its most outstanding features.

# Preface

When I was first converted in 1964 I was greatly impacted by the ministry of the late Dennis Clarke, a former Director of European Youth for Christ. Dennis left his native home of South Africa and came to reside in the United Kingdom, and with his friends Arthur Wallis and Cambell McAlpine provided an important teaching foundation to the emerging Charismatic Movement. It was at a Prayer and Bible week in Dennis and Beth Clarke's home that I first heard him refer to the extraordinary ministry of Pastor William Duma. Later, it was through Dennis that Pastor Duma came to visit Britain, and stayed for part of the time with me in my parents home in Bristol.

I will never forget the week I spent with William Duma. It had such a profound effect on my life and ministry. Whenever my parents and I reflected on his time with us, we could only sum it up in one way: 'It was like having Jesus in the house.'

Duma was a Zulu living in apartheid-dominated Durban, where he was pastor of the Umgeni Baptist Church. He had been President of the Baptist Union of South Africa, and came in 1966 as a delegate to Dr Billy Graham's World Congress on Evangelism in Berlin. It was after the Congress that he came to visit us in Britain.

I remember him as a short, but very powerfully built man, with the commanding presence that comes only from the anointing of the Holy Spirit. He was so quiet and un-demanding in the home, and when he preached he would whisper in one moment, then roar like a lion in the next. His preaching was so simple, and yet profound, focusing on the central truths of the Gospel; but when he prayed for people there was a wonderful blend of compassion and spiritual authority.

Of course, it was the astonishing miracles that accom-panied his ministry in South Africa that marked him out as 'different', and I'm so glad that Sovereign World have been given the opportunity of re-publishing this unique account of his life for a wider readership, but what was different about Duma was that there was none of the hype or extravagant claims often associated with healing ministries, even though he had personally witnessed most of the miracles attributed to Jesus in the Gospels, including at least two cases of raising the dead.

As a young evangelist, I drank daily from his wealth of experience. Some of the stories he told me are recorded in this book. Others are not, but there is one outstanding impression remaining from all the fellowship that we enjoyed. William Duma was incredibly attuned to the voice of the Holy Spirit, and remarkably obedient to His commands. One day, he was travelling by bus into the city of Durban and the Holy Spirit said, 'Get off the bus.' Although he was some considerable way from his destina-tion, Duma meekly got off the bus and began to walk. About a mile down the road he came across a terrible accident involving the bus in which several people had been killed!

Another story concerns a wedding he was asked to conduct. During the pre-wedding counsel with the couple, he became very uneasy about their suitability for marriage and urged them to delay their plans. However, the young woman was not about to be deferred, and they proceeded with the wedding service. Duma told me that he felt an unusual restraint of the Holy Spirit on the day, and instead of proceeding with the vows, began to preach. Ignoring the increasing restlessness of the congregation, and the agitation of the bride and groom, he continued for half an hour, then forty-five minutes. Suddenly, when he had preached for nearly an hour, the bridegroom fell to his knees and cried out: 'Stop the wedding – I'm a married man!' Few of us, I suspect, would have the courage to take such a radical step, but this implicit obedience to the Holy Spirit was the hallmark of his life.

I will never forget the day that he told me about an experience that changed the whole course of his life and ministry. Dissatisfied with his ministry, and desperate for a fresh anointing, he withdrew to a hillside near his home for prayer and fasting. On the third day, rising early, he walked up the hill and became engulfed in a cloud of shekinah glory. He was there for many hours, lost in the presence of God. When he came to himself, he was aware that the sun had set. He had been there all day, but there was no sense of time. As he walked down the hill that evening he said, 'Duma was a different man.'

After all these years, the fragrance of his life lingers on. Of one thing I am sure, you cannot read this book without your life being changed, and hopefully we too will become different men and women.

*Peter Lyne*
Auckland, New Zealand
1999

# *Chapter 1*

# The Herd Boy

*'His voice was like the sound of rushing waters.'*
(Revelation 1:15)

She stood on the brow of the hill, graceful as a gazelle, in spite of the full cotton skirt and tunic she wore. Scanning the gentle hills and quiet valleys of the Umkomaas, she appeared to be looking for someone. A Zulu woman, bearing an *ukhamba* of water from the river on her head, does not usually have much time to stand admiring the scenery! She was unconscious of the beauty of the fine morning, unaware of the deep calm of the hills. Lower down the slopes, hour by hour, a small Zulu herd boy sat in the shade of a large boulder. He sat, still and silent as the rock, gazing ahead, seeing nothing, looking for nothing, consumed with the wonder of creation. Suddenly he stiffened at the sound of padding feet. He turned to see the figure of a tall slender woman coming down a narrow path. She stopped at the boulder and, with the practice of the years, set her pot on the grass without spilling one precious drop. 'Son of my heart, how still you are! While other herd boys are playing at hunting and wrestling, my William sits, unmoving, while the sun hurries by. My child, what are you thinking about?'

'Oh mother! I look at the sky and think of the Great, Great One. I stare at the big mountain and wonder how it came there. It makes me frightened not to know. I wonder and wonder what God is like. How can I see Him? How can I tell people about Him if I don't see Him? My heart cries to itself. I am so lonely. Sometimes I long so much for *Unkulunkulu* that I think someone must come from the sky to me. Nothing happens and my heart feels as heavy as a stone. I also wonder, Mother, why your name is Nomvula.'

'My little ten-year-old, what strange ideas you have! Your mind is as busy as a bird in springtime when the nest is being made.

'Your mother knows so little. Born a heathen, married a heathen, it was not until I became a Christian that I was fed with wonderful words – words which made beautiful pictures to hang on the walls of my heart. My strange name, little one, was given to me because the night I was born a wild storm raged down these hills. It pelted on the thatch of the hut like the beat of war drums. When my first cry greeted the earth, my mother said, "I name her Nomvula."

'She was a prophetess. On each important day of my life, a door in the skies opened to pour down a sea of rain. It came on my marriage day in the church and on the day you were born. I think it will come again the day I go away.

'Fourteen years ago I came as a bride to the heathen home of the Dumas and had a heathen wedding. When I became a Christian, your late father, a kind heathen man, consented to our being remarried in church. What a day it was! The rivers were flooded and I wondered how I would ever get through them. I was terrified. But three strong young men, who knew every inch of the river, carried me across. Guiding themselves with stout staffs, up to their armpits in the water, they braced themselves against the force of the swollen river. I arrived at the church like a drenched bird – but even that is not the end of my rain story.

'The day you were born there was a flood. That day, the church people were having a picnic by the river and they had invited everyone who lived on the kraal\* to join them.

\* A village surrounded by a fence.

It was a beautiful morning and they begged me to go, but I refused because I knew you were coming very soon. I wanted to be alone to pray. I knew then, as I do now, that one day you will be a preacher. At dawn, with a heart in chorus with the birds, I went to the forest to cut wood for a fire and I carried water from the river. Then, alone in prayer, I promised God I would teach you about Him. I promised I would never stop praying for you. I sat alone outside the hut. The only sounds were the hens scratching for food and the call of a rain bird. Suddenly I felt cold. Looking up, I saw a bank of black clouds over the sun. Rain as heavy as stones peppered the roof. During that wild storm, William Duma was born.'

'My mother, our name Duma means "thunder" which also brings rain.'

'In truth, my *umfana*, waters seem to travel with us. It frightened me until I heard a white *mfundisi* read from the Bible about God's voice which is like "the sound of many waters". I was never again afraid! There is more rain story for you, but if I don't hurry with this *ukhamba*, I will never hear the last of it.'

The Duma home, cradled in the hills of Umkomaas, Natal, South Africa, was called 'The Big Kraal' and consisted of twenty huts and two large cattle pens. A kind old grandfather held indisputable reign. On occasion, his voice could rival the thunder of his name, especially when the women were troublesome. Into this closely-knit Duma family, Nomvula was welcomed as a bride.

In the second year of her marriage, one golden morning, Nomvula had stood between two sunlit aisles of tall mealies, their tasselled stalks towering above her. Enchanted, she listened as the wind rustled through the leaves. The morning's beauty obsessed her, luring her from work. Lifting her eyes to scan the hills, she caught sight of the Mkize kraal and at once a dark shadow came over her. Illness was there – a woman had been bewitched. Fear suddenly overwhelmed her. 'I could also be bewitched. Perhaps someone already has sprinkled evil medicine on the path I have to cross. Many are jealous of my good fortune.'

Fear was now riding her heavily. The day's tranquil joy had been killed in one stroke, leaving her a prey to the fears, superstitions and suspicions which dominated the life of her tribe. The Duma home meticulously observed the rites, customs, ceremonies and sacrifices to ancestors and consulted witchdoctors, medicine men and diviners in every kind of trouble or for advice. Below the lilting rhythm and carefree laughter of everyday life lurked constantly a note of fear. She turned towards home, her spirit in turmoil.

She met a stranger on the way and with customary friendliness they exchanged greetings and family histories. Nomvula invited the elderly woman home where they sat in the shade of a hut drinking *amasi* for refreshment. They were a picturesque contrast: the elderly woman dressed in black wearing the traditional *doek*, her hands misshapen from rough work, her face strangely, unexpectedly beautiful, and the young woman, her face signalling deep distress. Not knowing how or why, she poured out all her heart's agonies to the older woman. Thokoza, in turn, quietly related her history. She told of the death of her husband and seven sons, all of whom had died of tuberculosis. They had refused to go to the clinic or to be hospitalised. While they dallied with medicine men and witchdoctors, the disease was found to be incurable and they were admitted to the hospital to die.

As she listened with a frequent 'Hau' of surprise, Nomvula was struck by the suspicion that this woman had something others did not possess. She could not identify it, but she knew she had to find out what medicine or charms this stranger used to enable her, after all those deaths, to live alone in a hut at her age with eyes full of smiles and no complaints on her lips. Thokoza told her story of the day, now many years ago, when Jesus, the Saviour of the World, met her and received her into His Kingdom. Although illiterate, her speech sparkled, alive with love and with the fire of God.

Following that encounter, Thokoza visited the Duma home regularly until the infection of a new love had gripped Nomvula and she too was Christ's. This was the first flicker of light in the darkness of that heathen home. Instructed by widow Thokoza in the discipline of prayer, Nomvula was seen at the breaking of dawn, a blanket around her, going to her prayer hide-out. She used to say, 'The hens come down while it is still dark, but I go up to pray to send my spirit up!'

God was training a mother who would train a boy of whom it would be said, 'He is a man of prayer.'

It was now a year since William's mother had been surprised into tears at his haunting cry, 'How can I see God, mother?' Since then she had shared with the eleven-year-old boy everything she knew about her Saviour. Each night, the family, mother, two sons and two daughters, sat on their mats, by the wood fire, and studied the treasured pages of the Zulu Bible which William shared with his elder sister. No one could have suspected that the comfortable rhythm of Duma life was soon to be shattered – irrevocably.

Far away at the Kimberley Diamond Mine Uncle Vika had just completed his shift. He was walking to the store in the town when suddenly he came to an abrupt halt, rooted to the spot as if transfixed. In his mind he was transported to the hills and valleys of his beloved Umkomaas. In his ears he heard the lowing of the cattle; he saw the women around their cooking pots, the small scantily-dressed children tumbling over each other in the grass; he could smell the *amasi* and above all the drift of the smoke of wood fire. Slowly he realised that it was the smell of wood smoke drifting from an adjacent yard that had evoked these vivid memories of home, engulfing him in wave after wave of intense homesickness. That night a train was taking him east.

At that time of year it was customary to slaughter a beast to placate the ancestors by providing them with a sacrificial food offering. If this rite were neglected the family feared that the anger of the ancestors would descend on the kraal inflicting all sorts of disasters. They decided to await Uncle Vika's return which, unexpectedly, was that very night. But he brought with him something they did not expect at all.

Duma recalled, 'With Uncle at home the paramount question of the sacrifice to ancestors had to be settled. I shall never forget that appalling, disruptive night. As the family argued about the most auspicious date for the feast, they began to sense a strange, new quietness about Uncle. It was a separating silence, as if there was a strong antagonist present, dividing the family. Uneasily they asked, "What does our brother, so dumb there, say?"

'Vika replied, "I cannot join you in the feast. I cannot eat meat sacrificed to ancestors, nor drink the beer, nor have any part in the occasion. I do not believe our ancestors can bless or curse us. That superstition I have thrown away forever for I do not believe the ancestors eat the meat of the sacrifice."

'At this breathtaking renunciation, faces grew ugly with anger and fears. Words like poisoned spears jabbed the air until Vika raised his hand for silence, saying, "You want to know why? I will tell you. I have found the great secret which robs fear of its power. It isn't wearing goatskin around the ankles, wrist or neck, or sacrificing to ancestors; it is a power mightier than you know, invested in a Name, the Name of Names, and the Name is Jesus. From now on I am Jesus Christ's man. **He** is my Lord, Master of my life which is under His Kingly, Fatherly protection and love. When Nomvula came to this heathen kraal she was one with us. Then she became a Christian and brought us His Name, but our ears were suddenly deaf.

' "One day recently in Kimberley, a stranger came to me in distress. 'Tell me, Zulu,' he said, 'tell me if you know it, the Name of the God-Man who died for my sin. I have forgotten His Name, but He is in my heart. I'm going home to my heathen people. I must tell them of Him. He found me a few days ago. He died for me and my people must be told He loves them too.'

' "I told the old *mnumzane* His name was Jesus. He took both my hands in a grip of gratitude and walked away glowing, his old lips murmuring, 'Jesus, His Name is Jesus. I must remember, oh I mustn't forget, His Name is Jesus.'

' "Shame nearly drowned me and somehow my heart broke. I had tossed that Name here at home, but this stranger! I believe he would have forced his trembling spirit to stop everyone on the busy street, white or black, to learn the Name of the strange new lover in his heart.

' "At that moment Christ's love poured into my heart bringing peace and joy, and since then my spirit soars like the wings of a bird up and up surely to the gates of heaven. What is my secret? Jesus Christ is my Lord and Master."

'An ominous silence filled the hut, broken at last by a storm of words: "Get out, you and your family! We will not have snakes here. We will not offend the ancestors." Vika, seeing their once-loving faces distorted with anger and hate, knew he must go and go immediately.

'Silently he beckoned his wife and took her to their own hut. Then, alone, he went up the hill, past the prickly pears and aloes. He had been rejected by the family and knew there was no turning back. Sitting on the grass, on that merciful, tranquil, moonlit night, it took him a long time to realise his position. He knew that the boiling hate he had just experienced came from the kingdom of Satan. He marvelled that for so long he had been a member of that kingdom. Gradually comfort flowed from the realisation that against the darkness of sin which caused the rejection, was the dazzling glory of Christ's enfolding love for him. It warmed him like a blanket on a cold night. "Jesus," he whispered, "my heart has two rivers tonight. One deep and dark, flowing, for my people – one fresh and sparkling, full of peace and strength, a new river, buoyant to support me in this trouble. It must have flowed from Your heart into mine." '

In Duma's words, 'Uncle had a fever of God: he was mad with a first joy: the Name of Jesus was ever on his lips. Each dawn saw him climbing to a spot he made his prayer-home.

Visiting neighbours on the hillsides and in the valleys, his story poured over his lips like a river overflowing. The air began to be filled with unaccustomed gossip about a strange new subject.'

# Chapter 2

## The Call of God!

Vika immediately built a new home for himself and Duma's mother on the hill, naming it 'Elangeni' (in the sun). He combed the hills to tell anyone who would listen the story of Christ's love, making only a passing reference to his expulsion from the family when questioned. The community was completely baffled by his failing to seek revenge or consult witchdoctors to have the offenders punished. 'It is our custom!' they said.

The dimension into which Vika had stepped was unknown territory to them and intrigued them. They made excuses to visit him at the site of his new home. They were captivated by his daily life and in particular by his unique prayer hut. In a secluded spot high on the hill he earthed two straight strong branches with a space between and nailed a strong plank on top for a seat. This became his holy of holies. At nightfall he would go up to his sanctuary where, with a slow-burning branch lifted high above his head, he would signal to the heavens and anyone else who might see, that man was worshipping his God in prayer.

It was not long before the dark slopes were dotted with other flickering flames. Vika had learned that the only way to keep his faith was to give it away. From home to home he went, bubbling over with a joy that was infectious – a love that was all-embracing. Gradually more and more torches witnessed to the countryside roundabout that those

Christians were celebrating their holy hour of prayer. It was a mystical scene.

From the age of twelve to twenty, William suffered serious ill-health. Although he had committed himself fully to Christ in his fifteenth year, he struggled to come to terms with his illness and to find answers to his many questions. He slowly learned that he would have to surrender his question 'why' and lay it as a love-gift in the centre of God's will. These years of suffering, of unanswered prayers, of disappointed hopes of recovery, of waning faith were a hard training ground. He did not realise that his faith was being prepared for an extraordinary ministry dominated by an unwavering faith in the God of the impossible.

In addition to his persistent ill health, there came a day when his mother announced she was going to die. No coward soul, hers. Lying on the hut floor, she called her daughter to bring a piece of the straw they used for weaving mats, to measure her for her coffin. At that time, coffins were often made by a mission handyman or by relatives. Blacks would travel miles to obtain the *ibhokisi* taking two branches – one to represent the required length of the box, the other the width. With such haphazard measurements, it was not uncommon to hear the remains of a small body sliding from end to end of an ill-fitting casket. This Nomvula was determined to avoid. She insisted that the box be brought for her inspection. Satisfied that it was her 'fit', the children were called from school. Sitting up she issued instructions for their future. To her beloved William she said, 'My son, I want you to be an *umfundisi*, because that is what God sent you to earth for. Your uncle will look after you.'

As at her birth, marriage and the birth of William, so at her going, the sound of many waters accompanied her departure, the prelude to the trumpets that would greet her at the sunrise in the morning.

Between his fifteenth and twentieth years, William attended school and, when possible, worked in the store next-door to help support the family. He was deeply committed to the small local church and also to the welfare of the herd boys who affectionately called him *'Mfundisi'*. Faced with the problem of prolonged ill-health and a call to the ministry, the young Zulu had no bookcase lined with works on the mystery of suffering to help him, and neither was there anyone to counsel him. In his twentieth year, to resolve the dilemma of how he could preach while permanently ill, he decided to fast and pray for seven days. Each morning he left Elangeni for his hidden sanctuary with honeycomb, lemon and water for sustenance. Each sunset he returned home.

At the end of the seventh day, he left the quiet spot knowing that God had met him, that the wind of the Spirit had blown upon him – but had not healed him. Making his way slowly home, he turned to look at the place of blessing where he had hoped to be touched by God. It was there that the burning desire to be healed was replaced by a greater longing – that God Himself should be his only desire. Although his future was no clearer, he had gained one certainty, that he would not miss God's appointed destiny for him.

At midnight on the seventh day of his fast, unhealed, he got up to pray. His communion with God was so deep that the hours passed unnoticed. In the middle of the night, he felt a touch on his head and knew it was the finger of God. Heat like fire raced through his body, causing him to sweat profusely. He collapsed and, as he lay on the floor, he felt a surge of cold follow the heat and realised, almost incredulously, that the pain was no more. He described the moment.

'Although I knew God had touched me, I was afraid that the pain would gradually return. I placed my hands on the parts of my body which for years had been torn by pain. I tested and retested myself, then gathered my courage to see if I could walk without pain. I walked, walked faster, then stopped in a joy anchored in certainty – I was healed! Dumb with gratitude I knelt, knowing my healing was His charter for my life's work. In His good time, I had arrived. Solemnly

I made a covenant with God that each midnight, throughout my life, I would, as far as possible, keep an appointment with Him in prayer – a vow which I have kept by His grace.'

Following his healing, William went to Durban with a conviction that there he would find his life's work. He became cook in the boarding house of a gracious woman who, before her marriage, had trained in a Bible college in Scotland. Mrs M. Stewart, a Baptist and a woman of discernment, saw at once that the young Zulu was under the call of God to prepare for an unusual ministry. She recognised him as a 'free spirit', unfettered by customs, possessing humour, dignity and a good perception of the European mind.

She enjoyed telling how, when William heard her voice raised in family argument, he would creep to a point from which she alone could see him, with a mischievous smile put his finger on closed lips, shake his head negatively and slip away. She got the message to 'soft pedal'! He knew argument exhausted her.

William attended Bible classes under a gifted American missionary, Miss G. Hitchcock, who was in considerable demand at conventions for her expositions of Scripture. Mrs Stewart held daily reading and prayer with William and once a week a study group for black lay preachers, interpreted by a black teacher, met in her home.

While still serving in the kitchen, a modern Brother Lawrence, William took charge, as evangelist, of a small vigorous church under the American Board of Missions. He recalled his term of office there with great affection. It was during his time there that he was first used by God in an extraordinary healing.

One evening, a man and his nephew from William's home reserve at Umkomaas, knocked at the door seeking shelter. They were on their way to McCord's famous Zulu Mission Hospital in Durban because the boy, Msomo, had had an accident. While he was dusting he had knelt on a needle and cotton and it had gone right into his leg, although he did not seem to be in much pain. After prayer they settled to sleep but they were later wakened by the cries of the boy whose leg was in violent spasm. William described it, 'As I sat watching Msomo, a Voice said to me, "Why are you looking at the boy and doing nothing about it? Why are you not praying for him and with him?" Shamed into action I asked Uncle if I might lay hands on the boy. I did so, making it clear that the prayer was not for healing, but to give temporary relief from pain until they could get medical help.

'As I prayed the boy began screaming; his body stiffened. Pulling the blankets back he exposed the site at which the needle had entered. As I continued in prayer, the spasms stopped and, as if expelled by a powerful force, the cotton and the needle shot out of the leg! Amazed, we looked at each other speechless, and then began praising God. It was the very first time God used me as His instrument in healing.'

Modestly he added, 'I did not dwell on the healing, I thought it was just an isolated episode in my life, not to be in any way repeated.'

During his period of office as evangelist at the American Board church, William married Miss Grace Mkize of Umkomaas. Together they had three children, one daughter and two sons.

# Chapter 3

# Surrounded by Glory

'The Kingdom of Heaven is not for the well meaning:
it is for the desperate.'                    (James Denney)

The second healing in answer to prayer Duma did not assess
as an isolated episode as he had the first. Mrs Stewart's
daughter had been in hospital suffering from tuberculosis.
Nothing the doctors tried to do seemed to help and, having
been sent home to continue her treatment, there was no
improvement. Mrs Stewart said, 'William, I want you to
pray for my daughter's healing.'

After prayer he had his first assurance that recovery would
follow – an experience which was often to be repeated
throughout his ministry. Although not instantaneous, the
healing was complete and permanent. Mrs Stewart assessed
this healing very seriously. 'William, I believe God has
given you the gift of healing through prayer. Keep in His
very shadow and will, while He unfolds His plan to you.'

Shortly afterwards Duma received an invitation to
preach, with a view to a call, to a church – congregation
numbering seven! Inducted to the pastorate of Umgeni
Road in 1939, the new shepherd toiled, prayed and worked
for a year without any response. A deacon, 'with such a nice
face', was appointed to stand at the church gate inviting
men from the neighbouring factories to worship; handbills
were distributed to domestics working in the largely white

area in which the church stood; guest preachers were advertised.

At the end of the year the Pastor lamented, 'The church is on its deathbed, there is no sign of renewed life.' These were the words of a prophet and, like a prophet, he presented himself to the Lord, spread his complaint and took action.

He visited his friend and supervisor, the late Rev. W.N. Morrow Cook, then Pastor of the Bulwer Road Baptist Church, Durban. To him he said, 'Please don't have any more handbills printed, nor invite special preachers. No more will we try to lure people into church as a bird is coaxed into a cage with a cube of sugar. No, I'm going away, far from the track of man, to fast and pray for twenty-one days. The Holy Spirit tells me God will meet me there.'

In a valley near Hillcrest, a few miles from Durban, was a black community with a sprinkling of Christians known to Duma. There, at Emolweni, the Pastor hid himself. Daily he walked to the top of a lonely hill where neither man nor beast came – where only birds and an occasional butterfly passed. The first three days of his fast, Duma drank only water. Changing to orange juice and nothing else for the remaining eighteen days, he reported that his strength was fully maintained, his head clear, thinking easy – he was in perfect health.

Describing his vigil, Duma recalls, 'Each day, as I sought God, my spirit moved nearer to the Holy of Holies while God searched my heart unsparingly. Each day I saw with cutting clarity a vision of the kingdom of Satan. Everywhere I searched was the desolating, doom-laden word "sin". I knew I was being commissioned never to dally and parley with sin in my ministry. I was rather to expose it in all its hideous cruelty, to warn the sinner and to exhort the Christian to die to self.

'The twenty-first and last day of my fast dawned. Very early on that dark morning, I climbed the hill still wet with dew. Kneeling with my face to the ground I covered myself with a coat, for it was very cold. How long I stayed there I do not know, until, feeling suddenly very warm, I thought the sun must have risen. Raising my head, I found I was in the centre of dazzling light. A curtain of shining gold, suspended in space slightly above the ground, completely encircled my dark figure. I was confused with wonder as I discovered my body was glowing. My hands, no longer dark brown, were the colour of golden honey. Frightened, I slowly raised myself to peep beyond. It was still dark out there against the pre-dawn blackness. Only my hilltop was covered by the golden circle of light. Afraid to move, afraid to look and scarcely breathing, I waited until my spirit was suddenly freed from fear. Throwing off my coat, still kneeling, I praised and glorified God. Opening my eyes I found the glittering glory had vanished. Around the hill there was a new dawn accompanied by the homely, muted notes of sleepy birds. I thought, "The Lord is here and I am not worthy." With a sudden shuddering sense of the awesomeness of the Divine Presence I crawled away on hands and knees to the shelter of a boulder. I gazed toward the place where God had so incredibly revealed Himself to even me.

'At sunrise, I returned to the holy spot, rolled a big stone over to it as a memorial and sat on the grass, reliving the divine encounter. I do not know how long I sat there. All the earth was so hushed I seemed to hear even the veldt softly breathing as if in holy wonder.

'Then with authoritative clarity came a Voice soft yet strong, remote yet near, commanding as a King, assuring as a Lover, "My servant, you saw the tall cluster of white lilies growing so vigorously in the valley below: in just the same way your dead church will become a witness to me. You will see humanity transformed from darkness to light." After a short silence, gaining boldness, I ventured, "My Lord, please tell me if the healing of Msomo's leg had a special meaning for me?" Clear as the sound of running water below came the words, "My Son, I anoint you with the gift of healing. I charge you to proclaim the gospel of Jesus Christ – to perform in His Name the ministry of healing body, soul and spirit. I will be with you. I will not fail you." I knew the Holy Spirit had spoken.

'Long after leaving my Sinai, my spirit was still engaged with those spirits round the Throne worshipping, "Holy, Holy, Holy, Lord God Almighty." I did not know that, as I went back down the hill, I was totally framed in a silhouette of flame. Later, one Radebe told me he had waited that morning to offer me a small piece of ground on which to erect a hut for worship. On seeing the glowing light shining from me, he had backed away and went home greatly wondering. I was overwhelmed both by the commission conveyed so intimately by God to me, a herd boy, and also by that light, the divine signet on my life's work.'

During his hilltop retreat, announcements had been made in Duma's church that on the Wednesday of his return a five-day campaign would begin. The first evening the church was packed and there was a strong sense of the power of God. Scanning the congregation, Duma noticed, dotted through the congregation, five black women, each with their faces distorted under the power of evil. The awareness flashed through his mind that he had anticipated that, coming down from his hilltop, Satan might challenge his divine encounter in one way or another.

Simultaneously the women let out ear-piercing screams and rushed wildly to the doors. Men followed them to prevent them running madly into traffic or through fences, and it took several deacons to control the women's demonic strength. On Pastor's instructions they were led to the altar. He left the pulpit to pray with the sufferers individually, each supported by a deacon. Worshippers were instructed to kneel in prayer, all eyes closed, and Duma cried aloud, 'In the Name of Jesus, I command you demons to come out! There is power in the Name of Jesus.'

Following the classic pattern, as the demons were exorcised, each woman fell to the floor foaming at the mouth and lay as if dead. Each was possessed by more than one demon. Throughout the service they lay lifeless in the vestry, where they had been carried. Asked if he was concerned about their condition as they lay as if dead, Pastor replied, 'Not at all. I was bold in the Lord from my hilltop experience and had the assurance they were delivered.'

They awoke a little confused because of their where-abouts, but normal. Assigned to the care of friends for a few days, they were instructed in the faith. Of the five, three became notable witnesses to Christ's continuous power while the other two remained normal but 'on the fence' Christians.

During the five-night campaign there were over one hundred conversions. Day and night a crowd waited for prayer. The young people caught the vision of waiting on the Lord in prayer, and of waiting and waiting until they discerned His voice.

Duma's ministry began to develop rapidly and a number of strangers, beyond the confines of the Baptist church and the immediate locality, requested personal interviews and prayer. One such person was a distraught Jewess.

For years she had desperately wanted a child. Hope blossomed five times and five times she lost the infant before birth. Then the 'loveliest child in all the world' was adopted and there followed a brief spell of rapturous happiness until, in his sixth month, he died. She was inconsolable and close to a breakdown. Her Christian servant implored her mistress to send for her minister to pray to Jesus who answered all kinds of prayer.

She was furious. 'Who is this Jesus?' she roared. 'Even a white Gentile minister can't come here to talk about Jesus and you want a black one to come!' Celise crept beyond the sound of her wild anger, but gave herself to prayer.

Duma was packed and about to depart for Zululand when he received a telephone call from the distraught woman. '*Mfundisi*, I want you to come. Come this morning.'

'Madam, I'm sorry, I can't come, I'm just leaving to catch a train.'

'But I want you to come. You came to see my maid Celise recently, you greeted me, you must come.'

'Madam, I have urgent appointments, I cannot come today.'

'If you're a man of God you must come, I'm in terrible trouble.' A desperate note was in the voice – Duma cancelled the trip. He recalled:

'In the luxurious chauffeur-driven car, I was soon at her home. A frantic woman pulled me by the hands, sat me down and poured out her story. After some time I interrupted, "You want a miracle? You must give me a chance to talk to you. When an ill person consults a doctor, he does the examining and tells the patient what to do. You are the patient, you consult me. I must tell you what to do, but first there is something I have to tell you" ... and I knew there would be trouble.

'"Madam, I cannot pray for you except in the Name of Jesus Christ of Nazareth ... you want me to ask God to give you a child of your own. I must ask God through Jesus Christ His Son." At the sound of the Name, the orthodox Jewess stood up, grabbed my hands roughly and pointed to the door saying, "Get out of my house, otherwise I will call the police to throw you out."

'"Madam, you may call the police, but your maid is witness that you asked me by telephone to come here."

'She mocked, "Do you believe God has a wife that brought a child Jesus? That is insulting God. You're stupid, I want you to go."

'"As you wish, but I cannot pray to God only, breaking up the divine family, God the Father, Jesus the Son and the Holy Spirit." The Name which enraged her she repeated again and again with devastating scorn.

'"All right," I said, "let us put it off, but I am sorry to leave you because this Name is my medicine to cure you. I'll give you ten minutes. Go upstairs, I'll remain here, then give me your decision." When she had gone, I flung myself down on the beautiful Persian carpet, praying, "O God, I didn't call myself here, You did. Step in and break the ice of rejection and rebellion. This is the time to honour your holy Name." So I wept and prayed pleading the Name of Jesus.

'Hearing steps I arose. Unconscious of her disarray, she clutched my shoulders saying, "Yes, I take your advice."

'Determined there must be no compromise, I asked, "What advice?"

' "That you'll pray for me in the Name of Jesus."

'I pressed, "Do you believe He came to His own and they rejected Him?"

' "Yes."

' "You want me to pray for you in the Name of the Father, of the Son Jesus and the Holy Spirit?"

' "Yes."

'The husband was called at my request, a humble Jewish gentleman. "Before I pray, Sir, do you believe Jesus can heal your wife?"

' "Yes."

' "Do you take Him for a tonic for your body and soul?"

' "Yes."

'We knelt, Celise crawling to join us. The prayer was short. "Thank you, Lord Jesus, for the souls of this dear couple. Will you please provide them with a child and honour your blessed Name. Amen." I advised the lady to rest, while she insisted that I remain to lunch with her husband. I joined Celise in the kitchen. Together we beat up an egg and warm milk, and then we went upstairs to coax her mistress with refreshment which she took with a gentle smile. After my lunch with her husband, she reappeared, beautifully gowned, a new woman.

'What breathtaking commands God gives to His servants, even to me one of His least! Returning home that eventful day, I went to prayer. It was springtime in my mind. As I mused and meditated the Lord said to me, "Their faith must be nurtured, ask them to go to church with you tomorrow morning." I couldn't believe I had heard right. I implored God to confirm if that were really His command.

'I phoned them asking them to join me in church next morning. They consented. I sat between the couple as the preacher moved amongst the pages of the Old Testament, telling of the unrivalled faith of prophets, of their costly obedience to God, of their mighty deeds for Him. My new friend, the converted Jewess, whispered in my ear three times, "Isn't it wonderful!" A few days later they left for overseas on an extended business trip.

'My church was packed one Sunday afternoon. Two Whites, evidently missionaries, were squeezed between Blacks at the back of the church. After service, going to welcome them, I found they were my Jewish friends. They had come to find Celise and, above all, to tell me with faces and voices overflowing with joy, "The child will be born shortly."

'I was summoned to the hospital to bless the little man and choose a name for him. Thus the gift child, Peter Reuben, started his pilgrimage. Peter later always referred to me as "my" Rev. Duma.

'Most uncomfortable with a weightless little hat on my head I sat in the synagogue. I was moved to the depths by the Rabbi's address at the circumcision ceremony and later, at the feast of rejoicing at their home overflowing with guests, I was treated like a king. The parents took me to the study. In gratitude to God and to Celise for calling me, they had purchased a plot and were building a house for her widowed age. Education for her two daughters was provided at a seminary.

'Then they were offering me a cheque for £100 (R200). I put out my hand to take it when a Voice challenged me, "Who did the work?" I trembled, then falteringly explained I couldn't accept the gift for myself, the miracle was not mine. They were distressed until I reminded them how Elisha refused gifts from Naaman for his healing, and their hurt was changed into understanding. I accepted the gift for the church.

'When they left to settle in the United States, Peter Reuben had grown in favour and promise. I prayed he should be God's man indeed.'

# Chapter 4

# A Church of Prayer

The once dying church was now growing under the power of the Holy Spirit. Duma maintained his practice of returning once a year to Emolweni, where he had first been commissioned by the Lord, to spend time in prayer and intercession. During one such retreat, the Lord spoke specifically to him, 'Take the blessing of prayer I give you to the church, so that it witnesses to Me as a church of prayer. It is not enough to have the fire, it must be constantly kindled by prayer.' So, starting with three white women, Wednesday was established as the day for weekly intercessory prayer and healing services.

Duma urged all who attended the Wednesday sessions to fast from dawn to the close of the service which might be 3.00 or 4.00 p.m. To the eye of the visitor it was a church with a healthy pulse. Filled with a regular congregation, it was described as living and vital, and conversions and healings were accepted as the order of the day. Seekers of healing and spiritual help came from far and near to be present at the prayer services which became known throughout the Republic of South Africa.

Duma, however, was dissatisfied: 'Zulu that I am, I smelt smoke, a smoke that was screening sin, a smoke of satanic making.' One midnight, the time he had covenanted to spend each day in prayer, he laid his concerns before God. He received the reply, 'Be obedient to My leading and what is hidden shall be revealed.' He began to realise, through the Holy Spirit's discernment, that the service of Holy Communion was cold. He called a meeting of the diaconate and asked the six deacons to fast and pray on the Saturday before Holy Communion. After examining their hearts before God, if they found they were unfit to participate in the sacrament, he asked them not to officiate. One of the men fiercely opposed the Pastor's request, declaring that he and his wife would not comply. Duma replied, 'My dear brother, it is up to you, I have not introduced this by law or force. I am led by the Holy Spirit. I won't argue with you, you argue with the Holy Spirit.' There was a long silence before Duma closed in prayer.

At a meeting of church members a similar request was made. Duma sensed that there were some among them who took the bread and wine with a wrong motive, perhaps secretly hoping to bribe God to keep trouble away from them, in the same way they had once sacrificed a beast to their ancestors. Duma told them the story of how sacrificing to ancestors had kept his brother-in-law from being healed.

'Gumede was very ill with a chest complaint and his coughing kept the entire hut awake at night. Although a Christian for many years, he struggled to have faith for healing because he clung to his belief in the power of the ancestors to impose disaster. He was afraid not to make his offering and nothing we said could stop him preparing a sacrificial feast.

'Mother Shozi, the old widow who had endured much suffering and could truly be described as a "friend of God", had challenged Gumede. "Are you then so stupid that you believe that old heathen nonsense? That the spirits leave their graves to eat the sacrifice? Have you ever seen a grave open and spirits come out to eat? Have you ever seen the flesh of a beast eaten by anyone but a human? Yes, you might have seen it eaten by rats! Oh yes, I too was brought up in a heathen home. My people killed their beasts when the kraal had trouble, believing that it had been sent by the spirits of our ancestors who were angry because we neglected them. But Gumede, our Lord Jesus said to me, 'Shozi, My daughter, there's a place in My heart for you in which to shelter and dwell.' I entered that wonderful 'hut' and have lived there where no fear of ancestors, of being bewitched, or any of the witchdoctor's craft ever enters." Then standing tall with great dignity, like a prophetess she said, "Gumede, you poor sick man, wipe the picture of ancestors from your mind – take it right out. While it is there, how can you pray the prayer of faith? You can't. One eye is on God, the other looks to the ancestors, and you lie sick between the two. Wipe the picture out."

'After she had spoken, I prayed for his deliverance and healing. The Almighty One filled the room with His immortal power. Gumede never again sacrificed to ancestors. I urged my congregation to ponder Gumede's story. I challenged them to make sure they had on the wedding garment of God's forgiveness for all their sins before daring to touch the bread, or grasp the cup.'

When, on the Sunday in question, the deacons assembled in the vestry before the Communion service, one looked suspiciously uncomfortable. During the service Duma sensed the power of the Holy Spirit surging through the packed congregation. When the time for Communion came, Duma handed the bread to the six deacons seated around the table. As the deacon, who had refused to fast and pray, stretched out to take the plate of bread and touched it, he suddenly snatched his hand away, dropped the plate, scattered the bread and, screaming with terror, started kicking as if in a fit. Unable to walk, he was assisted to the vestry, groaning. Of the five remaining deacons, three refused to handle the holy vessels saying, 'The Holy Spirit is searching me'.

The church was in a state of shock. The people knew the affair of the deacon was neither incident nor illness, but divine encounter. God was in their midst in judgement. Some prayed; others were shadowed with nervous apprehension. A few refused to touch the bread and wine. Some whispered, 'I am not worthy.' There was a sense of the overshadowing of the Most High over the whole meeting.

The service over, Duma went to the vestry where the deacon was still in great distress. He admitted to hypocrisy and misconduct both in his work and in his private life and confessed that it had been going on for a long time. Weeping, he pleaded for the forgiveness of Jesus Christ, of the *umfundisi* and of all his fellow Christians. Duma summed up the impact of this incident: 'After the cleansing of the diaconate and church members by the Holy Spirit, the spiritual life and power of the church deepened most perceptibly. It seemed ever clearer to me that what Christians need – and need acutely – is a deep hunger for God.'

Blessings spilled over from the church into the most unexpected places – most notably on the church's next-door neighbours – the staff of a well-known hotel!

Late one night, the hotel's Jewish manager and his wife sought help to deal with some serious staff trouble. Guests' valuables and hotel stores were being pilfered by black staff. A bride was deeply upset having lost a valuable watch, a memento of an overseas honeymoon trip. Police had been called repeatedly; men had been punished, but the theft continued. The manager asked the pastor, 'Do any of my boys attend your church?'

'Not one,' he replied.

'Then it would help them to attend.'

'But their hearts must be changed.'

Duma had a suggestion: 'Ask your visitors to take their cars out of the large garage and tell your staff to put blankets on the floor. Instruct them to assemble in the garage and sit on the floor because I want to speak to them. Also, invite your white guests.'

What a scene! Youths and men tightly packed the floor, their black faces strangely pale in the electric light. Curious Whites filled the doorway. All faces were turned with questioning toward 'the little black man' who was to address them. There was obvious surprise when he announced he wanted to talk about customs. He related

*Take Your Glory Lord*

how Whites about to engage an employee used to inquire, 'What is your race?' If the reply was 'Zulu', they felt confident because they knew that the Zulu people were honest and trustworthy. Then he told them this story:

'I knew a white American missionary in Zululand. He wondered if the native people were as honest as they appeared to be, or whether it was a facade for ulterior reasons. He tested them by placing a pair of new boots on the main dirt road on which the mission was built. Each week hundreds of Zulu men and women travelled on foot, horseback, or ox-wagon over that road. He left the boots on the road for a week and spent much time observing the reactions of the travellers. He saw passers-by stop to gaze at the strange sight, a pair of new boots. They took them up and closely inspected them. They had prolonged discussions, surmising what they were there for and how they came there. They guessed at their cost and indulged in a great deal of mirth, but never theft. At the end of the week the missionary recovered them as shining and new as when he had put them there.

'Now,' he continued, 'our Zulu race has the Bible, education, places to train for a career, but no more honesty – not as in those days. Our race was trustworthy then. When a white master had to leave home on business, the kitchen "boy" would sleep in the kitchen to protect the madam and children. It was then common practice for a male servant to take a little girl, or one of his own age to school, sometimes passing through dense bush. He walked ahead as protector, she confidently, happily following behind. Now, we've lost the cream of honesty.

'You are not Christians and I am not speaking about Christianity, but about the old nature of honest Zulus – you all know why. You know, better than I, about the stealing – how visitors have been robbed as well as your employers. I am not here as a policeman, but as a servant of God to try to stop this evil. I want you to take my advice and do as I say.

'Tomorrow morning, the kitchen door will be opened at 4.00 a.m. It is winter and will be dark. Go in the kitchen:

you will not be watched, no one will be looking. Return everything that has been stolen. Put everything on the table. You will then not lose your jobs, nor will the police be called.' After giving them a short talk about the life of faith, he closed in prayer.

At 4.00 a.m. next morning there was a knock at the door of the room where Duma had gone to pray. It was the manager in his dressing gown. 'Pastor Duma, come now with me into the kitchen. The table is full of stolen goods, even to the watch of the bride – not one item is missing.' The two of them in dressing gowns walked through the dark to the kitchen. Looking at the packed table Duma knew the Lord had been working strongly in the hearts of the Zulu thieves. Later, guests and employees were assembled and were just as amazed at the sight of stolen goods spread on the table as if for a jumble sale. No one but God could have brought about such a miracle!

Addressing the company Duma appealed, 'Please no one touch anything until we have prayed. No policeman has helped us here, but the Great Detective, the Lord Jesus Christ, has found and returned everything, without the slightest hint of trouble. We will thank Him.' Then he thanked the staff for listening to the Voice in their hearts when he spoke to them the previous evening. As he prayed, it seemed that neither Whites nor Blacks breathed, so holy was the stillness that hushed the room against the loud clamour of early morning traffic passing by.

Duma asked the manager to release the black staff at 3.00 p.m. each Sunday afternoon to attend the church service, reminding him how often previously police had been summoned to no avail and asking him to think about what God had done. He agreed and there were a good number present in church. Over a period of time, ten of the staff were converted, baptised and became notable witnesses to Jesus Christ. Later, the manager and his wife spoke to a new Jewish manager of the miracle of changed personalities amongst staff following their conversion.

Each year amazing manifestations of God's power in healing followed Duma's yearly retreat at Emolweni. Through
unusual circumstances and God's wonderful artistry the
Holy Spirit brought together those whom Duma was
particularly equipped to help. In Canada a South African
Baptist Minister, the Rev. F. Mason, referred to the pastor's
healing ministry with the result that the man of prayer in
his humble cottage in Durban received a letter from a
woman in Canada, the contents of which were in English
and had to be translated for him: 'I am a very ill woman. For
eighteen months I have suffered from cancer of the breast.
Medical treatment has failed. I am a teacher unable to work.
I believe God urges me to write to you to pray for my
healing. I send a snap of myself and a blouse of mine, over
which please pray and then return it to me. I believe I shall
be healed while wearing it.' As Duma listened to the
contents he remarked that the celestial scribe must be
writing in the heavenly archives, 'O woman, great is your
faith!'

Praying over handkerchiefs was not new to Duma, but he
felt before he took the blouse to church for prayer, he must
seek God's leading. His doubts arose from what the devil
was steadily feeding into his ear, 'William Duma, this
person from a long way off has had many people praying
for her, including her own pastor, a very holy man, but with
no results. If you pray and she's not healed, what about her
awful disappointment, her smashed hopes?' When Duma
approached the Lord about this he received the reply, 'You
never asked her to approach you – her faith sent this blouse.
Do what I tell you – and that is ask Me.'

He took the Canadian request to the congregation.
Wednesday had become a synonym for prayer in the minds
of the people and for times of special visitation from the
Lord. Duma laid hands on the short-sleeved pink blouse as
though anointing her person. The power of God descended
mightily and he felt it soak the garment. It was returned to
her with instructions to wear it next to the skin and kneel in
God's presence for half an hour, then wear it trusting God.

Three months later a letter arrived and with it $100. 'The money would have gone to the doctors, I am not buying my healing,' she wrote. The church had been praying for just that amount to build a small church in Emolweni, Duma's hiding place with God.

# Chapter 5

# Pastor Duma

'To walk with God in the covenant of sonship is not a soft option.'                                    (J.A. Motyer)

Duma knew when he called a meeting of the diaconate to discuss finances, he would be putting himself in the firing line. He shared his conviction with the deacons that it was dishonouring to God and totally unscriptural to have concerts and socials to meet the church's financial needs. At most, those efforts brought a meagre amount which spelled perpetual poverty. For too long the church had taken its place in the queue, with other African churches, as beggars with an empty bowl for money from funds. Duma was convinced that there was something wrong with the spiritual life of a church which could not support itself. He challenged his deacons, 'Where is your faith? Is it so shallow that you ignore the promises of God? Have you one foot lodged in the world and one foot in the House of God? God's Word says, *"Remember this: Whoever sows sparingly will also reap sparingly, and whoever sows generously will also reap generously. Each man should give what he has decided in his heart to give, not reluctantly or under compulsion, for God loves a cheerful giver"* (2 Corinthians 9:6–7). Again, *"Give, and it will be given to you. A good measure, pressed down, shaken together and running over will be poured into your lap. For with the measure you use, it will be measured to you"* (Luke 6:38). My brethren, the spiritual intake of a man often governs the measure of his giving.'

As he spoke and studied the faces of his deacons, he saw a deep obstinacy written there. They made the inevitable reply, *'Mfundisi*, it is our custom.' Their faces grew darker and more shuttered as he spoke. The pastor deplored their little faith and declared it was an insult to God to adopt worldly methods, implying that Almighty God and prayer were inadequate to supply the needs of the church and family.

The popular way of raising money, described by Duma, was an extempore concert with a small admission fee. In a free and easy way anyone could call on someone in the audience to sing a song of their choice for which, with a final flourish, payment of threepence ($2\frac{1}{2}$c), sixpence (5c), even up to two shillings (20c) would be made. The last amount met with delirious applause. If the request came from a youth, the vocalist chosen was usually a girl. It often happened that before the song could be sung, one of the audience would object, pay for his objection and elect his favourite to render a different 'aria'! As excitement grew, feet stamped, exuberant communal singing dominated the arena and temperatures rose. Duma disliked those concerts intensely. Songs were often secular, with much swaying of bodies to the rhythm of tunes which, though suited to a dance hall, were out of place in a church. He was essentially a man of humour and fun who greatly desired amusement and enjoyment for his young people, but it must be wholesome – and not second-rate.

Ignoring their pastor's strong wishes on the subject of concerts, the deacons, with stubborn persistency, announced a 'coon concert' for the following Saturday night. Pastor was scheduled to visit his church at Umkomaas and would not be present, but he offered a silent, unorthodox, urgent prayer, 'Lord, please disrupt that coon show – even if they fight among themselves, deacons and all. Yes, even if the police have to be called, let it be so.'

Returning on Sunday afternoon he saw from a distance unmistakable evidence of disruption. Church windows were broken. The grounds were strewn with broken lemonade bottles which they had thrown at each other during squabbles. Deacon Twala went to meet his pastor with a very worried look and slow speech.

'*Mfundisi*,' (pause) 'we have great trouble' (longer pause). 'There was a big fight at the concert.' (I said to myself, 'Hush: keep quiet.') Twala proceeded, 'We were making tea in the vestry and fighting began. The kettle fell into the Primus stove which overturned and started a fire. Bottles were thrown about. We had to call the police.'

Other deacons joined the Pastor, solemnly deploring the damage. Pastor asked them to go with him to his house. They knelt to pray. Duma began, 'Lord, I have received sad news.'

'Hmmm: *au Nkosi*!' the deacons groaned.

'Thank you for the work you have done.' Deep-throated amens!

'Lord, what you have done is marvellous!' Fainter exclamations.

'Thank you for sending such chaos last night, for ending the concert with such a mess. Thank you for bringing to an end that which was grievous to You.' A silence of thunder!

Calling a deacons' meeting, Duma announced, 'Now we will start a new kind of concert. At the end of the year we will have a Day of Thanksgiving. Everyone will store away through the year a tithe of not less than R10.* There is no one who can't save R10 in a year. November will be the date for the first harvesting.

'When the time came I announced I would be in the church from 9.00 a.m. to 7.00 p.m. to receive the year's love gifts to God. By 11.00 a.m. I had not heard a footstep! By noon, one Indian woman came saying, "I give money." With slow fumbling, untying innumerable knots in her handkerchief, she at last discovered her precious offering,

---

* £5 (all currency values as at Duma's lifetime).

threepence! Bless her. There was talking outside and I thought, ah, here is a group – but they passed on. A heavy, manly footstep stopped outside – this is someone eager to pay his love tithe to God. Then I smelt the aroma of a pipe come through the windows – a man had stopped to light his pipe. The hours dragged by. I heard an army of steps which never came. One dear old woman brought her cherished sixpence. My wordless vigil was tormented by my old enemy, the devil. He looked at me, "Mmm", shook his head and said, "Where are the people?"

'By 5.00 p.m. the total income was ninepence ($7\frac{1}{2}$c). Said old Screwtape, "That's a wealthy collection you're getting", then a mocking laugh, "Duma, you're in big trouble." Desperately I said, "Lord, what is going to happen to show that you are a living Lord? It is now 5.00 p.m. and at 7.30 the envelopes are to be opened. Where are the envelopes? At 5.30 p.m. tea will be served."

'Then I started hammering on the Lord's door, "What are You going to do for Your glory? How are we to praise Your Name? I followed the leading of the Holy Spirit when I forbade concerts and bargaining in the church. What now?" Then my spirit there began to rise up to God as I heard the sound of many feet coming through the door and down the aisle.

'The service began while two white deacons opened envelopes. At last my people, in breathless silence, all leaned forward as if they were deaf, to hear the total amount. Oh, the intolerable waiting while the money was rechecked before the announcement of R200 for the Kingdom of God started a chorus of hallelujahs and praise which almost lifted the roof.

'That was the first victory. Umgeni Road was self-supporting.' Prayer and obedience had triumphed.

In 1975 R1200 was given on the Day of Thanksgiving.

When Duma later took on the role of Moderator of black Baptist churches over a number of years, he carried the vision of making the churches self-supporting into this wider arena. Wherever he went he urged the churches to be faithful in their tithing and offerings, assuring them that they would be joyously surprised and embarrassed with the heaping of God's blessing both upon the church and their personal lives.

## Duma Displaces a Deacon

Duma remembered another uncomfortable incident which occurred early in his ministry at Umgeni Road.

'I was a young unsuspecting, trustful pastor. Anxious to visit outstations, I did not hesitate to leave a Sunday service in the hands of the senior deacon. Past middle age, he spoke as one used to authority, with frequent, appropriate references to the spiritual life and church work. From his tongue rolled a vocabulary about God and prayer that would have done credit to a travelling evangelist. It was a great relief to me to know, as I journeyed to Amanzimtoti to preach for the first time in a church under my charge, that all was very well at home base.

'Returning to find the afternoon service still in progress. I slipped into a back seat. The senior deacon, as arranged, was conducting the service, but, as I looked, I wondered if my eyes were focusing right. Had the deacon acquired a peculiar mannerism when he preached? Swaying from side to side as if obeying a secret rhythm, I wondered if that was his style or a Pentecostal touch! More and more, as I listened intently, I was nonplussed, embarrassed and finally sweating. As he continued, I became more and more confused. To make the situation worse, there also appeared to be a practice among the women of whispering to each other while the preacher spoke. I wondered anxiously what kind of a church I was shepherding. Uttering a prayer for myself, I walked towards the table below the pulpit. I took the speaker by both arms, led him to a seat and sat him down. I pronounced the benediction. After the service he called the deacons together. "Tomorrow," he officiously announced, "we shall have a special deacons' meeting. I expect this dog to come." The dog was I. Deacons and the Dog duly met.

'That man had been chief deacon for very many years. I was new, young, inexperienced. Moreover, his employer was a well-known senior deacon of a local white Baptist church intimately connected with Umgeni Road. He was also a man of influence and affluence!

'Next day the offender's employer telephoned me, "I have known this man for many years. He has been a great help to the church. You had no right to do what you did in front of the church people who respect him. He has been a senior servant in my home for many years."

' "Sir," I said, "the man was drunk. I am the minister in charge. This man may be a very good chief in your kitchen and over your servants, but he is not any good in or for my church."

'I attended the diaconate on Monday pondering many things. I took my place as chairman. The senior deacon arose and said, "You come out from that chairman's seat." He instructed another man to occupy the chair and said to me, "Up", with a corresponding gesture.

'I replied, "Sit down. I want to face you tonight. If I'm not moving from this church, you must move. We will settle this tonight. I am certainly not going, it will be you who must move. Thank you meanwhile for calling me a dog. For your words you must go. I also ask you, 'Who called you to be a pastor of this church?' "

' "I have been called by the church."

' "Have you been called to be a deacon or pastor?"

'The offender replied, "I have been appointed senior deacon. When there was no minister I did everything."

' "Quite."

'Offender: "What right had you to march up the aisle and remove me from my pulpit?"

'Pastor: "My right was the authority of Scripture. The Temple of God must not be defiled – and you defiled it with your drunkenness. Did the other deacons stand by you?"

'A scornful "haa" was his eloquent reply. One deacon to whom I addressed questions hummed and evaded the issue saying, "I didn't notice he was drunk." Another, anxious to retain the goodwill of the offender said, "I didn't see he was drunk." Twala, dear faithful Twala, stood up and boldly declared, "I do remember he was swaying as a drunken man. At first I was puzzled, but when *Umfundisi* removed him I knew my suspicions were confirmed. The women behind me were all commenting on his intoxicated condition." Another deacon, given courage by Twala's stand said, "It was right for *Umfundisi* to remove the senior deacon as he did. We were in the House of God – such insult to God could not be allowed." Twala then confessed, "Some time ago I was put out of office because of certain wrong-doing. I confessed my sin. I accepted my period of discipline and later was re-elected to the diaconate." Twala appealed to the offender to acknowledge his guilt and say "sorry" to the Pastor.

' "Oh no, Pastor must say sorry to me."

Still pleading his cause of righteousness, the deacon in the dock took up a Bible, threw it at the Pastor's face and broke his glasses leaving a splinter of glass which just missed his eye and lodged in his cheek. He then walked out. Twala wiped the blood from Duma's face. The meeting closed.

The offender occasionally attended church in the style of a big chief – always in the seat of the scornful, breathing out his vicious antagonisms. Finally his boss's wife took him to Duma to apologise.

'His "sorry" was reluctant and unwilling. He weighed an apology to me in the balance of her wishes and continued approbation in the household in which he had been the Chief for thirty years.'

Pastor Clifford Nxumalo took up the story. 'I knew the household where the deacon worked. Members of the household staff were told, "That is not a good church at Umgeni Road. They have a pastor who likes to turn things upside down. Or "I don't know where the offerings and tithes go. Always there will be a white man at the back door of the church – he comes with a bag and takes all the money – what does he do with it? That money has been given by the Africans! He takes it to feed his own children." All he said came from red-hot hate as blazing as a bush fire.

'His final ambush was to make friends with a deacon in charge of an outstation. "Why," he demanded, "are you so foolish as to take the offerings to Umgeni Road? Why take them? Don't you need money? You could buy a plot of land."

' "There is no need to take to Umgeni Road money which is given to a white man to spend on himself. I have been a deacon for a long time. I know what happens with the money. Keep it until you have sufficient to buy that plot for yourself."

'The deacon capitulated to the evil suggestion. Mysteriously and suddenly very little financial support reached Umgeni Road. Ultimately it was discovered that together they had hoarded £80 (R160), which by then had disappeared. Appalling trouble fell upon that deacon's house and his family.'

✤   ✤   ✤

In 1946 antagonism, secret and open, was decimating the work of God at Umgeni Road. One of the more obvious causes of the resentment was the fact that the Pastor would not consent to his children attending social concerts, cinemas and other gatherings which he considered were unsuitable to and harmful for them. The criticism was so bitter that an assault on his person was planned.

One morning a black car was parked under an old tree near the gate of the church. In the car were about six young black men between the ages of twenty and twenty-five. Duma, in his church office, was unaware of the car's presence. The young men, while still in the car, asked one another who was going to lay hands on 'him'. They knew that Duma's name was known throughout Natal and that he was very well respected. The first man said, 'No, I'm not going to do that.' Another said, 'But we have been paid, we must go and do the business.' Yet another declared, 'You go, I am not going to touch the man.'

'Well then, what are you fellows going to say to the man who has paid us?'

'I don't know. I can't lay hands on him and I'm not going to either.'

'What are we going to do? Do you realise that we each have cash in our hands? We can't take cash and not finish the thing.'

Finally one of them said, 'Gentlemen! If we are not going to do what we pledged, let us just drive away and forget about it. We will tell the man we failed to find *Umfundisi*.' Confused among themselves they drove away. Through it all, Duma worked on in his office blissfully unaware of the danger outside.

# Chapter 6

# A Blaze of Glory

*'I am the Lord, the God of all flesh, is there anything too hard for me?'*                                    (Jeremiah 32:27)

[Jesus said], *'With God **all** things are possible.'*
                                    (Matthew 19:26)

It was in the late 1940s and Pastor Duma had just returned from his yearly pilgrimage to the hills, where he had spent many days alone with God. He felt renewed and was acutely aware of the power and presence of God. His joy was, however, suddenly shattered by devastating news.

Bhengu, a middle-aged Baptist evangelist in a rural area of Zululand, rang to tell Duma of the tragic death of his seventeen-year-old daughter, Litta, who had died the previous evening after three weeks' illness. Bhengu, a man of great faith, had prayed and fasted for his daughter's healing. During his intercessions, he had felt unmistakably led by the Holy Spirit not to send for medical help – he must trust God utterly. Duma never opposed medical help. On the contrary, he would suggest it whenever he felt it was appropriate. Again and again, Bhengu sought the Lord on this point, but each time received the answer, 'Trust **Me** only.' Now Litta lay, a corpse, on her mattress on the floor. At the end of the telephone, Duma was stunned. He too had prayed, but now the brightness surrounding his prayer and the encouragement his faith had received, was a black blur.

As the girl had eaten less and less and her condition had deteriorated, Bhengu had felt more and more convinced that he should put his trust in God alone. Despite the protests of family and friends he felt he dare not, he could not, disobey the mysterious command which he was sure God had imposed on him. According to the rural law, the police were notified. They closely examined the corpse and issued a death certificate.

Duma left Durban immediately by taxi for the burial. He was dropped five miles short of his destination. Trudging the remaining miles he became suddenly conscious that his dejected spirit was being lifted up by the Holy Spirit. Inexplicable joy overcame his grief, and he began to praise God the Father, the Son and the Holy Spirit. He realised also that in his spirit he was making an incredible request to God, that Litta should be resurrected from the dead to the glory of God. As he passed through the countryside, a barrage of insults were fired at him from workers in fields, from women at their cooking pots, from passing horsemen and pedestrians. To all these he was not only impervious, but unaware. Nothing pierced the depths of his communion with God.

The district was offended because no doctor had been called. They howled, 'Is that the teaching of your church? You should be ashamed.' Cocooned in God's presence, he pressed toward the end of the journey where he was joined by two companions, who had been waiting for him. Mrs Magwaza, a woman among women, whispered in words reminiscent of Bethany, '*Mfundisi,* if you had been in prayer, Litta would not have died.' Jali, a humble saint of Duma's church, walked unnoticed, in silence by Duma's side. As they approached the house of mourning, muted singing wafted towards them. It was a favourite hymn of comfort, 'Remember, the home over there'. The relentless sound of spades, the cutting of earth as the grave was being prepared, was a grim accompaniment to the hymn of hope. Duma walked on seeming not to hear, head uplifted, as if in another dimension, seeing no one, greeting no one.

Entering the home, he walked through the rooms crammed with people to the place where Litta lay rigid on her mattress on the floor. Closing the door, permitting only the parents, Jali and Mrs Magwaza to remain, he examined the corpse to make certain for himself that she was dead. Ice cold, no pulse, no heartbeat. Jali, versed in the tribal tests for ascertaining death, said, 'She is gone.' Experienced Mrs Magwaza confirmed his verdict. Duma had seen and examined too many corpses to have any doubts. This was no coma – Litta was dead.

In the room of death, Duma was strongly under the power of the Supernatural. The four onlookers sensed his total engagement with an unseen Presence. Instinctively they drew aside and stood against the wall. Whatever he was experiencing it was totally beyond them. They saw, not their beloved little minister, self-effacing, with a quiet voice, but a man clothed with a new stature, invested with an unearthly authority, far removed from them in spirit. Calling for a basin of water and small towel, Duma gently bathed the face of the girl. For him time was no more. Silence curtained the room. Standing, he silently anointed Litta with oil. Suddenly he sank on his knees beside the mattress. He was unable to stand any longer. Still kneeling, he took the girl's hands, clasped together in the unyielding clutch of death and, with tremendous wrenching, separated them, placing them widely apart. He then lay, limb to limb on the body, as Elisha had done, but not with mouth to mouth. Years later, describing the experience, his voice subtly changed, as if again becoming aware of the mysterious dimension in which he had moved at that awesome time: 'I prayed a few words in my own language, then I lost my "humanity". I was no longer a person. I did not know what I was saying. I spoke, not in other tongues, but beyond tongues. I was unconscious of a mind, a brain, or a thought. I was away from the body, totally in the Spirit and yet I cannot tell how. I forgot everything – who I was – what I was – where I was – what was happening. I know only that I called in a voice louder than my own, a voice somehow reinforced, "Litta!"

'Almost immediately, I felt a strong movement against my breast, a pushing, which grew stronger. I rolled off the body, onto the mattress and further to the floor. I was incapable of standing. I turned to look at Litta. There was a slight movement. We watched, scarcely breathing. Time seemed to stand still as, unaware that we were watching, she raised, or it seemed that she was being raised very slowly, inch by inch, until she lay upright against the wall, her startled eyes unrecognising, unmoving, unknowing. I tried to stand. I longed with all my heart to run from that house, from that room, away, away from the power of the presence of God which was too "intense". It overpowered me. But I could only crawl on my knees. I could not stand. I was sweating profusely. Someone picked me up, carried me to a bed, gave me a change of clothes. For three days I could not lift my hands, nor walk. My only sustenance was pawpaw or *amasi*. I was carried to a car for home where, for two weeks, I lay in bed, my son, Enoch, feeding me. For three weeks I saw people in duplicate and was totally powerless.

'I learned later that Litta, after a time, had been fed two teaspoons of milk at intervals by her younger sister; her parents were too shocked and even scared to enter the room. It was seven days before she could crawl slowly on her knees, holding onto the wall. When it was first known that Litta was sitting up supported by the wall, those who had come to comfort the family, fled. Later, they were allowed to pass the open window of her room in single file. They moved in awed silence to see she really was alive. Still later, people from near and far gathered each night over a period of time for services of praise and thanksgiving in the home.'

For Pastor Duma this supernatural experience was deeply awesome. He said, 'Although evidences of the strong surge of the Holy Spirit in our midst have moved me to depths and heights of speechless worship, yet I never, never want, in the flesh, to pass again through the dark caverns of the glory of that day.' He continued, 'There was an "afterwards" when God visited me and said, "Duma, My servant, you sit down in the dust for the rest of your life. That which you have seen and heard was granted to you because of your great faith and humble spirit. Beware of pride, watch and pray, lest Satan destroy you with its poison." The effect of this indescribable experience on my ministry was a greatly reinforced faith and depth to my spiritual life. *"All things are possible to him that believes"*, was now deeply engraved in my spirit.'

While Duma was, 'he knew not where, but out of the body', Litta was in a place she could not describe – a place with a 'shining of light' so very beautiful. She saw the Lord who beckoned her to come to Him, stretching out His hands towards her. Lovingly, He led her to a viewing point and bade her to look right down. She saw Duma stretch himself upon her. As Litta watched the drama, the Lord said gently, 'Daughter, you must go back there.'

After her recovery, Litta accompanied the pastor to white and black churches to tell of her experience with a solemn joy. Before her illness she had been noted for her devotion to Christ. After her supernatural ordeal, she was clothed with an influence which moved congregations to tears. Often in women's meetings, hands would be raised for her to stop, the lifted veil was more than they could bear. Her voice had a poignancy as if she remembered a beauty she had seen and lost. Her face was often radiant through tears. From that sacred time in the uncrowded Presence of God, Duma shrank from casual reference to it – his holy of holies must not be sullied by cheap talk.

As the story of Litta's return to life filtered through to Durban he was besieged by newspaper reporters, as he had often been. He maintained his rule to refuse all publicity – to God alone was the glory.

## *Chapter 7*

# New Horizons

On God's calendar, the time had come for Duma's ministry to spread. In 1947 he had a significant dream which God used to open up new horizons for him, eventually including Britain, Scotland, India, the then Congo, Zambia, Rhodesia, Swaziland and also the International Congress on Evangelism in Germany in 1966.

When Duma awoke one morning, having dreamt that his children were playing in the garden unaware of a poisonous snake in a bush, he knew it was more than a dream. Later in the day, seeing the children there, he took a hoe and searched the branches but found nothing. Positive that his dream had meaning, as he continued to search, he suddenly disturbed the snake in the roots of a shrub. The snake rose up, poised to strike. In this extremely dangerous situation Duma's predicament was to avoid the attack of an angry head, while grappling with a hoe to cut through the lower portion of the long body partially hidden in the earth. The hoe he used was not noticeably sharp! It was a battle to the death with a very sweaty Duma the victor. The reptile measured six feet, its poison was lethal.

When the Superintendent of his church, the late Rev. Mr Morrow Cook, heard about the dream, he invited the Pastor to share it with the congregation at Bulwer Road Baptist Church, Durban. Very reluctantly Duma agreed, 'Because of my English.' In 1948, when asked to address the white

Baptist Assembly, the problem of his poor English again came to the surface. He protested, 'I can't do it – my English is very poor. I cannot speak polished English.' His refusal was not accepted. Eventually he took the language bugbear to his sacred retreat at Emolweni, where he threw his 'unpolished English' into the lap of God. If any doubts remained, they were dispersed forever during his first services to white and coloured churches in the Cape, where he held a campaign at the invitation of Rev. F. Mason and preached to a packed hall night after night.

There were also bonus surprises.

On their way to Fish Hoek, Cape, where Duma was scheduled to preach, Rev. Mason took him to a young footballer who had been injured while playing. Lying on a bed with protective rails, the young man lay paralysed from the waist down and could not speak. His gentle mother had been his companion for seven years. Shocked and filled with compassion, Duma took off his shoes, climbed over the rails of the cot and knelt as close to the sufferer as possible to give him the strong assurance of nearness and love. Duma then embraced and anointed him, asking Mr Mason and the mother to rotate the limbs very gently while he prayed. Later he acknowledged that he did not know why he had made the request to exercise the limbs. As they said goodbye, Duma noticed the agitated efforts of the young man's lips, as if he were desperately coaxing the breath in his throat to vibrate the vocal chords. Then, with a supreme effort, he whispered, 'Goodbye.' A loud sob rent the room as his mother cried, 'That is the first sound he has made in seven years!' The recovery was slow, but very sure. When completely recovered, he went to Rhodesia to work. Strong and radiant, he remembered with deep gratitude all that the Lord had done for him.

With faith running at high tide in Wynberg, as the campaign drew to a close, Rev. Mason and Duma were called to the home of a coloured family to pray for a small child of two years of age who had been born hideously deformed.

Duma described the meeting. Entering the room invigor-
ated and excited by all the Lord had been doing at the
recent services, he was taken to the child and was immediately taken aback. Born in hospital, the child had remained
there for months before being discharged. Medical science
was baffled and helpless. She lay with knees up to her
shoulders, each frail foot touching her cheek, the left foot
on the right cheek, the right on the left. Shocked, Duma
looked at the parents, searching their faces. Did they really
believe the bundle of displaced and distorted legs and arms
could become normal? Theirs was a history of long, patient,
agonising waiting, holding onto the hope that somehow,
sometime, somewhere, prayers would be answered. They
had waited for so long for this decisive moment of prayer.

Duma had experienced so much of God's miraculous
power that doubt had seldom troubled him, but now, at
the sight of the child, his faith was ravaged and doubt
mushroomed as he continued looking. The devil seized the
opportunity. 'How can you change God's will? You're
tempting God. Now you're faced with the impossible.'

The Holy Spirit countered, 'God allows you to glorify the
Name of Christ.'

Duma reported, 'I listened until Satan nearly converted
me to complete doubting. Then, as I ate his words, a sweet
voice broke through with the strong words, "I am the Lord
that heals" – take that promise.' As I leaned hard on the
promise of God, I was overwhelmed with the assurance,
"Now the Lord will heal through the man." Then, like a
flash of lightning, faith and power flooded my whole being,
my tongue was set free and I interceded for the child. At
9.00 p.m., that night I left for Durban. Three months later,
the little two-year-old was walking and the parents felt like
kissing each footprint in the sand in gratitude to God.

## Belgian Congo

Duma was invited to preach at a campaign among mine
workers in the Belgian Congo, now Zaire, which was

experiencing a strong move of the Holy Spirit. White and black ministers shared the evangelistic outreach which was held in the stadium of the black township, where workers gathered after 5.00 p.m. Duma invariably preached while the remainder counselled. One evening, after an altar call, a member of the South Africa General Mission asked Duma to counsel an African who refused to be dealt with by a White. He was a member of the Mau Mau, from Kenya, who under great conviction told his story.

'I will have no white skin to counsel me. I was brought up on a mission station with Whites who were very kind to me and whom I loved. They educated and cared for me until I left to work – but my grandfather died as a result of being beaten to death by a white farmer. When I see a white skin, bitter hatred rises in my heart choking me.'

Duma prayed and counselled with no response – nothing could penetrate the man's bitter heart. Duma protested that because one White had sinned against him this was no reason to hate all Whites, forgetting the flow of love he had enjoyed through many years of white kindness. That was not a fair balance. Finally Duma reminded him that we are all sinners – that was why Jesus came to die on the cross, to forgive us **all**. Scripture says, *'Forgive, and you will be forgiven'* (Luke 6:37), and *'. . . forgiving each other, just as in Christ God forgave you'* (Ephesians 4:32).

Suddenly the man broke down and wept bitterly. After the service he went to the mine office to tell the Whites of his conversion. The press insisted on photographing the converted Mau Mau. Publicly he spoke of the hate he had nursed in his heart for many years. For all the joy he now experienced in companionship with his Lord in prayer, there was always a haunting note of lingering sorrow in his voice for the irretrievable wrong he had done as a member of the Mau Mau. Its appalling harvest of death was something he continued to travel with. 'It seems,' he said, 'as though I took a large pillow full of feathers to the top of a very windy mountain, opened it and scattered the contents to the far corners of the land. Then someone said, "I'll forgive you if you can bring back all the feathers" – and I knew that only God could bring back to me all those feathers.'

On three subsequent visits, Duma met this man who, although he could not bring back the feathers, flamed his way through life proclaiming the burning love of God's forgiveness.

## Rhodesia

Invited to Baptist churches in Northern Rhodesia, now Zambia, Pastor Duma described the embarrassment of being assigned to counsel two Whites. The occasion was a convention for Whites, youths and adults, lasting three days and nights which was being held at one of the largest farms in the district. Rev. A. Erasmus, then minister of Kitwe Church, arranged for Duma to preach on two nights. Just before his first service, Duma was told, 'One of our **big** men is coming tonight. He is an important scientist lately returned from the United States. A lady doctor holding a prominent position in a hospital is accompanying him.'

Duma tells the story. 'When I heard all this, my spirit sank. I said to the Lord, "If You don't honour Your lovely Name at this meeting, it will be flat and it will be Your affair."

'The Lord replied, "I stand with you, throw out your fear."

'Courage reluctantly took over. That night I gave the address and the altar call. Shaking hands with those dear people I walked down the line to the "big" man and his friend and commended them to God. Then came the shock. Pastor Erasmus, allocating counsellors, said, "Duma, go to the couple on the chairs under the tree." They were the Big Man and his friend.

'I refused. "No! I can't, that is your job, you have a BA degree!"

'He quickly countered, "You have a BA (born again) from the Lord."

'Again I stubbornly refused, till with a lightning stroke of illumination, I realised I must take my cheap pride, throw it out and humbly obey God. I grabbed my Bible. The saliva in my mouth dried up. My tongue stuck to its roof, my words also had dried up. I crawled along so slowly that my shoes hit one another and it was a long, long way to reach them taken inch by inch!

'I confessed to them that I had asked Pastor Erasmus to counsel them and that I was thankful they had gone forward without hesitation, but said I would like to ask each of them the same question, "Why did you go forward?"

'The Big Man replied, "When you preached, Jesus became a new Person to me. He came alive and walked out of the pages of the New Testament, because your words were so practical and I love to hear a practical message. You told of healings and other episodes which showed Christ's intense interest in the everyday affairs of men and women. You haven't borrowed your message from anyone else, it is your own experience. It imprinted itself deeply on my heart and mind."

'The doctor expressed the same convictions in her own way. I prayed with them.

'The Big Man was gloriously Christ's from that night. Years later, on a return visit to Kitwe, he came from Ndola to greet his spiritual father, the little black man, Duma.'

## Scotland

After attending a Congress on Evangelism in Berlin Duma travelled by air to Glasgow where he was the guest of a heart specialist, Dr Kelly. He was given a warm welcome by the handsome Scot but after the Pastor had rested, the doctor carried his son of eleven years to see him. The young lad, who was suffering from a serious heart condition, was very pale, blue veined and excruciatingly thin. They had a conversation about healing, but the doctor did not ask him to pray for his son and Duma didn't push himself.

Dr Kelly took Duma to various meetings, including one at a Pentecostal Tabernacle. Duma takes up the story, 'Oh, the hallelujahs that were going around. The doctor with his Scottish reserve was a little embarrassed, but I enjoyed them.

'He was of the Plymouth Brethren persuasion and, through his influence, a meeting of ministers of the Church of Scotland and other denominations was organised at which I was to speak. There were fifty-five of them. The young minister in the chair, I was told afterwards, had nine degrees! The meeting was held in his church. I said to myself, "Who am I, this little Duma, speaking to all these academics? I have no polish in English!"

'The Lord said, "Duma My messenger, listen, I am with you." Then came, surging through me, the power of the Lord. As I spoke I counted at least five men in tears. The young man, loaded with degrees, of whom I had been so nervous, wept. At the close of the meeting the young chairman, instead of returning me to Dr Kelly's home, pleaded that I go to his manse for lunch. He was a lovely young man with a very fine spirit.

'One morning, Dr Kelly instructed his chauffeur to take me to Edinburgh to see the Castle. As we drove through Princess Street my heart was saying, "It is a long time since I saw a black face. I have seen thousands of these nice white faces, but sometimes I long to see a black face." I called to the chauffeur, "George, I'm dying to see a black face."

' "What do you mean?"

' "Never once since I've been here have I seen a black face."

' "Are you not happy with us, Pastor?"

' "I'm as happy as a fish in water, but I long to see a black face." Then I cried, "George, go back, you passed a black face. He's standing in the rain under an umbrella at a bus stop. Please reverse, George."

' "I can't do that, it is against the regulations." Eventually he reversed. I shouted a Zulu greeting, *"Sakubona."* He didn't understand. "Good morning. Good morning, come here." He came. "Where are you from?"

'"Jamaica."

'"Hau! I'm from South Africa." He shouted, "Get out of the car, let me see you from South Africa." I got out. We hugged each other we were so glad. I asked, "Are you a Christian?" "Yes." "What church?" "Baptist."

'Then Baptist Duma and Baptist Jamaican embraced each other and exchanged addresses. "Goodbye."

'"Goodbye" followed me in the car as we moved on.

'Following the ministers' meeting, it had been arranged that I should speak at a Tabernacle in Glasgow which seated 1,500. It was scheduled for 8.00 p.m. Sunday night, after the churches had finished their services.

'The young minister had taken me to his vestry wardrobe to fit me with a gown, because the gowned ministers of various churches were to be on the platform with me. He tried one after another of the gowns, each with academic colours. I said I couldn't wear any of them. Eventually I went to the platform in a Geneva gown. The choir was singing. It was nearing the time for me to speak when suddenly I was in great distress with severe pain in my heart. I got up to speak but was forced to lean hard on the speaker's desk, bent forward because of the pain. I called the young chairman minister to come to me. "I am sick." He looked stunned, maybe also a little dubious. "I am sick. I have discerned there is someone in the congregation with a very bad heart complaint. You must announce it and ask the man to come forward." He looked at me, at the congregation and hesitated. "Look," I said with sudden authority, "I am a man of prayer, you must announce what I ask."

'Looking over the packed building he called, "Excuse me. Pastor Duma has discerned that there is someone here with a leaking heart. It is not a recent disease but of a few years' standing."

'Right from the back came a cry of a great distress, "Oh, Lord, it is I."

'He stood with his wife and I said, "That is the man. Come, brother, you are the man."

'He cried, "I can't walk."

'Four men carried him like a cabbage. I left the pulpit and nearly fell, still in pain. A little lady caught me and helped me to a chair. As soon as the man came, I grabbed him to my bosom and called, "Everyone here lift up your hands." Then aloud I cried, "In Jesus' Name, to the glory of God, I claim this man's healing."

'The sufferer caught hold of my arm and cried, "Praise the Lord, praise the Lord. I am healed, oh, I am healed", while he walked up and down the aisle, up and down as though he would go on forever walking up and down because for so long he had not walked. A tremendous wave of power flooded the Tabernacle, bursts of praises soared up to the very roof and I was filled with the fire of the Holy Ghost. My pain had ceased immediately I had embraced the sufferer. I began to preach, "What shall I do with Jesus which is called Christ? What will you do with Jesus which is called the Christ?" but the message was never finished. From the galleries and from the aisles, people streamed to the front.

'Dr Kelly, my host, the heart specialist, and two heart specialist colleagues were sitting in that congregation witnessing the work of the Physician Jesus. The healed man had been a patient of Dr Kelly and his colleagues for some time. Immediately we reached home Dr Kelly came to me, "Pastor, I want you to pray for my son."

' "Why?'

' "Because in that service I saw what God could do."

' "But your son must be prayed for in a public meeting that the glory of God shall not be hidden."

'My next service was in a Baptist church. Dr Kelly carried his son there and he was prayed for. The next morning, early, the little lad, Howard, brought coffee to my room, scarcely able to believe he was walking.'

# *Chapter 8*

# The Power of Discerning Prayer

'Pray absolutely for those things you may pray for absolutely. Pray conditionally for those things you may pray for conditionally. For those things you can't pray for – don't. Always will in His will.'

(Paul Gerhardt)

One night during a campaign in Ndola, in the territory then named Northern Rhodesia, now Zambia, the queue at the altar was so long that those asking for prayer were divided into seventy groups. Pastor Duma passed down each row asking, 'What is your request?' One young African girl, with words tumbling from her lips in desperate eagerness, explained that one of her legs was shorter than the other. It was in callipers. She pleaded for prayer to make it grow. Expressions of expectancy and doubt contended with each other on the face of the pastor's specially chosen assistant. A breathless mixture of trembling faith and unbelief rose from the congregation as they waited for the pastor to speak. His simple prayer was interrupted by the sound of the girl's voice, 'I'm healed! I'm healed!' Her excitement hindered the removal of the callipers. As soon as she was released, with arms outstretched, she ran round the church, up and down the aisles, her dress fluttering behind her. The congregation, ashamed of its doubt, praised God with laughter, groans and tears. Her father, a Member of Parliament, answered a telephone call to come at once. Hardly daring to believe the news he flew in from Lusaka to witness his daughter's joy as she explained, 'Jesus came to church to stretch my leg.'

Two black youths, both over twenty, who witnessed the healing conferred together. 'This man,' they said, 'is not a Christian, he is a witchdoctor.' The more they discussed it, the more convinced they became that it was not God who had worked the miracle. They planned that on the following night they would join the queue at the altar, simulate a disease and trick the trickster.

Pastor Duma vividly recalled that they were sixth and seventh in the row of those kneeling waiting for prayer. As he approached them, he saw that they were surrounded by a threatening black cloud. He related, 'My spirit was immediately angry. My tongue stuck to the roof of my mouth. I had no words whatever to pray for them. I beckoned a minister to take them away at once and counsel them. I reported they had come to mock and try to trip me up. I realised this was satanic interference and announced to the congregation they were not ill. They refused to be counselled, became difficult and left the church shouting in a language no one understood. One ran to a neighbouring village and knocked at a door for refuge; the other collapsed. The last we heard was that one completely disappeared and the other went insane.'

Discernment had a prominent, central place in the life and ministry of Duma.

> 'The man without the Spirit does not accept the things that come from the Spirit of God: for they are foolishness to him, and he cannot understand them, because they are spiritually discerned.'                    (1 Corinthians 2:14)

One morning a white woman with a little girl arrived at Duma's home carrying a cryptic note from a German doctor. 'Dear Rev. Duma, this case is not for me, it is yours.' No hint of diagnosis was given. The worry of the mother's heart was etched indelibly on the still young face. 'No one,' she said, 'has been able to give me help or hope.'

Duma discerned it was a case of demon possession. He assured the puzzled mother that Jesus still had power to cast out demons. At first the child resisted all approaches by the pastor but through the power of the Holy Spirit, who was in total control of the situation, the little girl was soon sitting, contented, on Duma's lap while he called upon the Name of Jesus to exorcise the demons. One by one, reluctantly, they left the child. She put her arms round the pastor's neck, nestling close to him, content and at peace. A little later she remembered her mother and turned to look at her. Immediately Duma observed waves of terror passing through her small body. Looking to discover the cause, he saw a brood of six dark figures in a semicircle waiting, unabashed and defiantly, to re-enter the child. With a commanding voice Duma loudly commanded the demons to return at once to the hell from which they had come. According to Scripture (Matthew 16:19), he bound them, forbidding them ever again to trouble the child. From time to time the radiant mother brought the pretty growing girl to greet the man who had obtained this freedom for her in Christ.

Asked how he could diagnose the difference between a case of mental illness and demon possession Duma replied, 'I have no difficulty. The Spirit of God clearly reveals to me the difference and long experience has made it easier.'

✢  ✢  ✢

## A modern Gadara – a woman among the tombs

In a black reserve on the south coast of Natal, she was known as the mad woman. Like the man of Gadara, she lived in a cemetery, where food, and clothing which she usually discarded, was placed on the graves for her.

One brilliant Sunday morning the harmonious singing of a congregation was suddenly disrupted by a piercing cry, like that of a wild animal. Nearer and nearer swept the uproar. The worshippers turned round to see a wild woman, scantily clothed, lurching up the aisle towards the pastor. Deacons immediately jumped up to intercept her but Duma cried, 'Don't touch her, leave her to me!' Taking the struggling woman, her strength trebled by the force of the demons within her, he called with the voice of authority, 'In the name of Jesus of Nazareth I command you to come out of this woman!'

Three times the apostolic command rang through the church. Collapsing on the floor, foaming at the mouth, she lay as one dead. On the Pastor's instructions she was carried to an anteroom where a woman stayed by her side. The simple hall was enveloped in the glory of Christ as worshippers experienced the spell of the mystery and the majesty of His presence.

Over an hour later the preacher was concluding his message, when quiet, controlled footsteps walked up the aisle. '*Mfundisi*, may I speak?' It was the woman from the tombs. 'I don't know in what dark and terrible country I have journeyed for years, but I know Jesus has healed and brought me back home. My heart is crowded with words I can't utter.' She stood in front of Duma, her calm face glowing. Overcome by the Holy Spirit's presence, he stood silently before her. The eyes of the congregation focused intently on the two figures at the table. Duma, still silent, was communing with his Lord, 'O most lovely Christ. I now see the truth of your eternal words, *"Behold, I make all things new".*'

After the benediction, the deacons inquired why the pastor had commanded them so sternly not to touch the demon-possessed woman. He explained that demons are free of the kingdom of Satan and go in and out seeking human habitation. 'I take no risks with Satan. I pray Jesus to cover and shelter me with His blood. I have known many instances where, in pride, men have presumed to deal with demons in their own strength with disastrous results.'

One such case was a black family from Johannesburg – father, mother and two children – who were all very ill, trekking from one doctor to another, finding no relief. Wherever they travelled between African huts, homes and clinics one name kept cropping up – Duma. 'You must go to Durban, he is a man of prayer.'

So it was Pastor Duma found himself confronted with this family of four. He described the father as a man of personality whose voice was like the growls of a disturbed animal of uncertain temper. He discerned a severe case of demon possession in each member of the family.

After prayer, which always preceded exorcism in his ministry of the Holy Spirit, demons visibly came out of each member of the family in turn. It transpired that the father was a leader of a Zionist sect which had a very large following amongst the Africans. He had exalted himself to the status of healer, had placed his hands on demon-possessed victims with the harrowing result of the family's near destruction, he being the first to be invaded. He was not a Christian, was untaught in Scripture and prided himself on his prowess.

✤　✤　✤

Pastor Duma, conducting a mission in the Cape, received an urgent request by telephone to visit a town to pray for a man who had been in a coma for three years. He would be taken and returned to his mission base by aeroplane. Duma felt compelled to go and immediately prepared himself by intercession.

Arriving at the hospital, under the Holy Spirit's pressure, Duma made an unusual request – to see the white doctors. With surprise on their faces, the medical men listened with astonishment to what the Pastor had to say, 'I have not come to pray for the patient's healing. God forbade me that. He will soon receive the divine summons.' They urged, 'You must see his wife. For months, without hysteria, she has made a death vow if he goes.'

Duma recalled, 'I was taken to where, in a car in the grounds, she was waiting for me. She told me of her decision to destroy herself and her two children if her husband died. I gently told her of God's plan for her beloved, as revealed to me in prayer. God wanted her husband for Himself and desired her to let him go on his journey with all the lovingness of her heart. She must not spoil his going by one bitter drop of her rebellion. Her face hardened. Again I pleaded but received total rejection. I walked away, I know not where, agonising in prayer. I returned to search her face, her eyes, but they were as hard as marble; to listen to her voice to catch a softer tone, but it remained defiant. I prayed and talked with her, only to walk away locked in prayer. I do not know how many times I approached her, to listen, sympathise and pray. Elijah, in his day, prayed seven times for rain, looking again and again for the smallest sign of a cloud heralding the rain. This I did for two agonising hours.

'In distress, I cried to God as I came to speak to her for the last time. She surprised me by a sudden explosion, "All right, I'll let him go." I helped her out of the car and led her to her husband's room. I placed a chair for her close to him at the head of the bed where she could see the face she loved so dearly and touch his hand on the bedspread.

'Family and physicians were called. I opened my vial of oil, explaining that it was not for his healing, but to anoint him for his passing to see the King in His beauty. As I anointed the dying man, I was acutely aware that the room was throbbing with the warm, sweet, tender Presence of the Holy Spirit.

'His wife, yielding to the will of the Most High God, was breaking her life's most costly alabaster jar of nard, her tears flowing as if in holy peace for all her heartbreak – her face, for all its pain, strangely suffused with tender beauty.

'As I was praying aloud and began to say the benediction, I looked at the sufferer and saw he was making an effort to lift his hands slightly as if in blessing. When I came to the amen he shaped his lips to say it with me silently. Those were his first conscious movements in three years. By nightfall, in Paradise, he had seen the face of the Lord he loved.'

## Chapter 9

# Three Women Are Healed

She had travelled through years of darkness and sorrow –
now she had come to Pastor Duma to share her story.
Young Mrs Rebecca James, graceful in her sari of autumnal
colours, told how she had lost, one after another, four
premature babies. For this gentle girl, married at seventeen,
living with the loss of these tragedies and the specialists'
dark prognosis, the future looked bleak. But despite her
losses, she still held onto a faint hope that she might yet
have a child – but the hope was overshadowed by the
devastating question, 'Would it live?'

At last, under the watchful eyes of the specialists, a full-
term baby was born – but born with six fingers, six toes, a
cleft palate and a cracked skull (meningocele). With the
baby in intensive care, Rebecca, quietly weeping, prayed for
a miracle. Compelled to go to the little one, she looked
down on the baby's tiny crumpled face which seemed lined
with pain. Stumbling, through her tears, back to her bed,
she prayed for two hours that it should suffer no more but
be taken – a prayer swiftly answered. Momentarily tempted
by the tablets at hand to end the prospect of a childless
home, she was afraid to question her Lord – she was a
Christian.

Much later in time, desperate with anxiety because,
against all medical advice, she found she was again pregnant, she heard of the Umgeni Road Prayer Circle. Although

a member of the Full Gospel Church, she decided to attend
the next prayer meeting. Pastor Duma made an appointment with her for 7.00 a.m. on the day of prayer.

Duma recalled her visit. 'Her story was very heavy, her
spirit was deeply troubled, her past medical history threat-
ened her prayers and her thinking, but shining through the
mists of fears was a resilient faith.' Touched by the anguish
of this young woman, now five months' pregnant, the
pastor asked the Lord how he could help her. 'Give her
encouragement!' came the reply.

'Just as you give a hungry person a bottle of milk to
sustain him, I gave her a bottle of encouragement in the
Name of the Lord. I told her she must regularly attend
the Wednesday weekly prayer meeting. She never failed to
arrive at 7.00 a.m., hours before the scheduled time. I
covenanted with God and her to fast and pray for seven
days from sunrise to 2.00 p.m. At first my prayers seemed to
hit boulders of obstruction and return sterile to my spirit. I
persisted in prayer and pressed on in the dark for some
assurance from God that a healthy child might be born.
There came to me a vision revealing that the skull of the
babe she was carrying was broken (meningocele) as in her
last child. On the sixth day of my fast I had a vision of a
frog, the head just a little open. I wept in brokenness before
God pleading, "Holy Father, it mustn't happen again, oh it
mustn't – husband and wife once again to be heartbroken,
please my Lord, not again."

'Then in vision I saw the Lord had commenced knitting
the skull together. I partially explained to the husband the
condition of the foetus and God's assurance to me.

'It was then totally unexpected when during a Wednesday
morning service Rebecca suffered an untimely crisis. My
gaze was suddenly directed towards her, sitting in a comfortable chair in the prayer row. Deep signals of distress were on
her face. It was her eighth month, the fateful time when she
had lost her other babies. Immediately I summoned women
to form a screen around her. The full church immediately
went to prayer of their own accord.'

The intrepid man of faith went into swift action. Placing his hands on the abdomen and realising that the foetus was in a transverse position, he prayed, 'O God, take these unskilled hands of mine and guide them by your Holy Spirit's power.' Direction and power came to his hands, but their movements were against a strong opposing pull of satanic interference. 'The strong force of Satan tried to dislodge my hands,' Duma explained. 'In the Spirit I grabbed his hands and again cried aloud, "In the Name of Jesus and on His holy authority I bind you, Satan! Take your dirty, filthy, interfering hands off mine!"

'The opposition grew stronger and I repeated my command, my voice growing louder and louder until at last I felt the undisputed power of God guiding my hands and was assured that the foetus was now in normal position. I saw peace, indescribably beautiful, pass over the face of Rebecca. Then I knew and the church knew, and I felt that the angels knew, that the Physician of Galilee in all His loveliness was in the church with us. Every head and all hearts were bowed before the Presence which dispersed doubts and healed disease. Rebecca went to rest in the vestry.'

In due time a perfect child was born. Rebecca continued to make each Wednesday her special time when she left her growing family for the Prayer Circle to kneel in prolonged prayer and thanksgiving to the Lord who met her in her deepest need.

✢ ✢ ✢

For three years Pastor Duma had been receiving letters from Dannhauser, Natal, asking him to go there to pray for a sick woman. Then an urgent letter arrived, stating that taxi expenses would be met! Chuckling, he remarked that to offer to pay for a taxi must mean it was serious indeed! He told the story.

'Dannhauser is a long way. I didn't know the people and I was very busy. I prayed that if I were to go, God would give me a sign – the sign was to send someone with whom I could travel. That very day a European railway missionary friend, whom I had not seen for some time, arrived. I asked where he was going. To Dannhauser! Silently I thanked God. Then Mr Devil tried to interfere. "Don't be a fool, Duma. Let them pay your fare. You'll go that long way by rail; the woman won't be healed; your congregation will hear of it – what a scandal for the cause of God and what an ass you'll look! You'll never again be able to pray for the sick." I replied, "Satan, if you talk like this, then I know this is a big *indaba* which will bring glory to God."

'Looking out of the train as we neared our destination, I noticed a red brick cottage, its garden full of peach and apple trees in fruit. At the station, the husband of the patient clutched my hand and wept bitterly. He led us down a narrow path to the gate of that delightful cottage. He told of his wife's fruitless journeys to hospitals and specialists. The skin condition had been diagnosed as leprosy, but later tests were negative.

'Listening to the harrowing case history, we reached the gate when Satan said, "You'd better change your plans before it is too late." The husband preceded us into the house. I halted with one hand on the gate and said to my missionary friend, "Let us pray." I felt the Person of Christ so vibrantly near that I held out my right hand to His invisible Presence, saying, "Please, Lord, take my hand and lead me to victory for your Name's sake." I felt an anointing of the power of God upon me so that I walked into the house as if I were a giant, short as I am.

'The sharp cries of a woman in pain filled the house. I asked to be taken to her. She was in bed, her hands and arms a mass of gaping sores. From a bag at her bedside she took chips of bones which had splintered from her arms. The stench filled the room. "*Mfundisi*," she whispered, "I lie here saying why does God do this to me? Why doesn't He answer my prayers? Why?"

'I told her I would pray for her but I must be sure she had no accumulated rubbish in her heart which would obstruct God's power. "Mother, have you been lying there full of rebellion and bitterness? If so, confess it. I see you have called in the witchdoctor and medicine man, and the bones have been thrown. Although you profess to be a Christian, you have trusted the evils of Satan." She confessed to all those sins.

' "Husband, have you harboured in your sinful mind the thought, why does this woman go on living? It is time she died. My comforts are all gone." With tears he admitted he had paid much money to the *inyanga* to slaughter beasts for the ancestors and to smell out the cause of the disease. Confessions over, I called for a basin of warm water and a towel.

'Taking the arms rotten and offensive with disease, I placed them in the basin. Slowly I washed fingers, hands and arms again and again. The only sound in the room was the drip, drip of water from my cloth and the plop of brown pieces of sloughed skin, as they fell into the white bowl. The devil suggested, "I told you what a fool you were to come here – you will contract this infection – the woman's disease will fasten on you." "In the Name of Jesus, be gone!" I countered. Cleansing finished, a heavy stillness filled the room. A train lumbered by. I offered a short prayer, thoroughly cleansed my hands and left her. Suddenly I was overcome with unspeakable weariness and asked to lie down. In a small room I slept for two hours until I was called to lunch.

'Hearing footsteps coming from the garden, I saw a woman with a bowl of fruit hurrying up the path. For all the assurance God had given me, my eyes suffered from unbelief! There she was, radiant, only dry scars on her arms as evidence of her earlier diseased condition. Offering me the fruit, she said, "I planted those trees. Eat of the first fruits and make thanksgiving. I'm healed, all pain gone, I am new."

'When the homeward train passed the cottage, she was vigorously waving both arms calling, "God is great, I am healed." Her Zulu was sweet on my ears.'

✢  ✢  ✢

Mrs Francis stood in the doorway of the rectory in night-dress, dressing gown and slippers awaiting the return of her husband, the Rev. J.W. Francis, Rector of St Aidan's, the large Indian Anglican church in Durban. He should by now, she argued with herself, have concluded the three services of Ash Wednesday morning. Mrs Francis had suffered over four pain-packed years during which she had, with depressing monotony, entered and left St Aidan's Anglican Hospital, of which her husband was chaplain. There had been specialists' consultations, experimental treatment, hopes, disappointments and much endurance, throughout which she was no better.

Reviewing her case history it is not surprising that she was desperate. Her disease was an enigma. Each prescribed cure had failed. Despite prayer there were times when death hovered. Honesty compelled her to acknowledge that at that time she was spiritually dead, although, paradoxically, she called on the Name of Jesus during attacks, with no belief that He could heal in spite of the prayers on her behalf.

Into this desperate and hopeless situation came an Indian nurse with a story to tell about her father who had been crippled by an accident, hospitalised with serious spinal injury and discharged incurable in a wheelchair, with crutches for occasional use. He was taken to Umgeni Road Prayer Circle and carried to the front where the sick waited. Pastor Duma prayed and anointed him. He took two steps with crutches and, feeling the surge of new life permeating his whole body, threw them away and walked up and down the aisle while the congregation held its breath as he returned radiant to the front.

The healed father travelled many miles burning with joy to tell Mrs Francis the story he had now related so many times. 'If you go to Umgeni Road Prayer Circle with faith, what the Lord did for me He'll do for you.'

'Those words,' she said, 'quietened my restless, fretful, disappointed heart. I accepted the evidence of his statement and said, "I must go." But I had a problem. My husband had said, "None of these so-called pastors will lay hands on you. I must be faithful to my Church." Then he had added humorously, "We will give you a loyal Anglican burial." '

On that Ash Wednesday morning, she had telephoned Pastor Duma's church and learned there was a Prayer Circle that very morning. That was why a desperate wife stood at the front door awaiting her husband's return. When he arrived, he remonstrated that she was not fit to go, but finally conceded to her urgency and determination. 'It shall be well,' she insisted in reply to his objections.

So, Mrs Francis arrived on Ash Wednesday morning with her husband at Pastor Duma's church assured, 'It shall be well.' Her nurse took her forward to join the prayer line, but was stopped because the quota was complete.

Conspicuous in his black robes for he had not had time to disrobe, Father Francis slipped into a back seat to hide, feeling very embarrassed. Meanwhile, learning of the urgency of the case, the Prayer Circle nurse and counsellor had placed Mrs Francis at the end of the queue. Reaching the last two in the line Duma announced, 'I cannot pray for any more healings. The Holy Spirit has told me to stop. If I pray now it will be in the flesh and useless.'

Mrs Francis, though not prayed for individually, was included in the mass prayer and advised to return the following week. She realised the pastor was right not to have laid hands on her without an interview. In the car returning home, Father Francis said, 'You didn't get any help.'

'What! Haven't you noticed my hands aren't shaking now?' Her husband conceded that, 'The type of healing I saw was scriptural, I approve of that kind of ministry. It will give me great joy to go to that man to make an appointment for you.'

Taken into a small prayer room at Duma's home, Father Francis was kept waiting a long time. 'I was very tired,' he said describing his visit. 'There came a whispering, "Why don't you go away? Don't waste your valuable time", a temptation I'm glad I resisted. I felt very strongly that I must accomplish the purpose for which I had come, although I feared my reception might not be cordial since Pastor was so long in coming. When at last he came, he extended his hand and smiled, and immediately I felt the warmth of his friendship and love. My heart was touched.

'An appointment was made for my wife to be the first in the prayer line the following day. When I arrived at the church, the pastor did not allow me to sit hiding at the back, but took me to the front seat. As he was preparing to lay hands on my wife for prayer, he suddenly stopped and announced, "There is a woman in the church in great pain in the womb. Come forward, I will pray for you." No response. The call was made three times, his voice ringing with authority through the surprised silence. A timid woman, bent double in pain, slowly came forward and was prayed for. Immediately relieved of pain and walking upright, amazement lighting up her face, she returned to her seat.

'Then, turning to my wife, Duma quoted, " 'I am the Lord that heals you.' Do you believe that?" '

Describing that moment of encounter with the supernatural, Mrs Francis said, 'I couldn't speak. I cried and the tears were of joy and sorrow mingled. I knew this was the destined moment in time when the Lord was going to touch me.'

As Pastor Duma laid hands on her for prayer she collapsed and fell to the ground. Supported by a pillow, she lay unconscious for fifteen minutes. Pastor, undisturbed, said she had without doubt been attacked for some time by an evil spirit. When consciousness returned, she described her condition as being born again. Hers was an instant healing, that is, all pain and distressing symptoms were completely gone. Strength was restored gradually.

Commenting on his wife's healing, Father Francis said, 'The most fascinating thing was that God used her healing to revive my own ministry. God led her to Umgeni Road, not only for bodily healing, but her entire personality was transformed and my ministry resuscitated. My own people noticed the difference in the presentation of the gospel. They felt they were really and truly fed with the Word of God. Church attendances considerably increased and the parish benefited generally. My people knew we had gone to the Baptist church and that I had an intimate friendship with Pastor Duma. We both attend his Wednesday Prayer Circle in which I actively participate. We also attend the Sunday afternoon service. At Umgeni Road, they not only preach the gospel, but richly enjoy the fellowship of Christ and His Holy Spirit. Being among them is contagious. It is easy to feel that Christ walks from pew to pew and that He is alive in their midst, invisible but not intangible. The gospel I preach is dynamic because I myself am living in a new dimension.'

# Chapter 10

# Changed Lives

## Our Girl

Pastor Duma was travelling to visit the Zionist community on the south coast, several miles from Durban. Taking along with him Jali, his Zulu comrade, the two men boarded a bus one Saturday morning in order to reach their destination in good time for the first service which was scheduled for 2.00 p.m. that afternoon. The bus, which was full of shoppers, stopped, not only at appointed places, but anywhere on the country roads which might save a passenger a walk. Old and middle-aged African women, mostly of heavy build, alighted with much caution; the driver helped, there was prolonged thanks and family gossip, all of which delayed the bus considerably. By noon, Duma and Jali had not arrived. On and on they travelled through the afternoon until, at 9.00 p.m., they were shocked to discover they had arrived at the terminus.

'But this is not the place we are visiting,' they told the driver. 'When does the bus for that area leave here?'

'Not before tomorrow afternoon and I am not going to the place you name.'

To their dismay the driver suggested that perhaps they had taken the wrong bus. He was right. Seeing a vehicle in Durban at the place from which they were told the bus would depart, they had taken their seats, asking no questions. Nine hours later they were at journey's end!

They looked at each other aghast: 'The congregation has been waiting for us since 2.00 p.m., and no one can tell us where Kwa Mthambeka is, or how to get there.' Jali suggested that though the night was dark they should walk along the verge of a dirt track until they saw a light or heard a baby cry. With this faint hope and a suitcase slung over each back, they walked through the darkness from 9.00 until 11.00 p.m. Eventually, they saw a dim light in the distance. Knowing that the local custom prevented them from knocking on a hut door so late at night, they walked to the centre of the kraal precincts and called out loudly, 'We are friendly travellers.'

The owner replied, 'Who is there? Where do you come from?'

'We are lost. We come from Durban.'

'Hau! Where are you going?'

'To Kwa Mthambeka.'

'Oh no, that is too far from here. What are you going to do?'

'There is only one thing we can do: we'll try and find a place where we can wait for morning.'

'I can take you for this night.' The owner then appeared and took them to a hut, lit by a small paraffin lamp, where he was roasting meat on a fire kindled on the floor. The host announced that he was an African Congregationalist which is a community who have no Whites. Near the roasting meat was some alcohol. 'He was that kind of a Christian,' Duma wryly commented.

While the host was calling a servant to make tea, Duma whispered to Jali, 'We have come at a good time: he is roasting meat and we are hungry. Meat roasted on a fire is food fit for kings.' On his return the owner removed the meat from the fire and took it to another hut! The servant then led them to their sleeping hut. The aroma of the wood fire mingled with the tang of the meat made their mouths water. They awaited the return of the servant with that roast meat. She arrived with tea and two dumplings made of mealie meal, customarily served with roast meat, but they were raw! As soon as they were out of the way their host returned the meat to the fire!

In the morning they were given a little water to wash their faces but no refreshments. Anxious to get to their waiting congregation, they were directed vaguely towards a river through which they passed with water up to the thighs. Thirsty and hungry, with no prospect of food, they trudged on until 1.00 p.m. Sunday – they were already twenty-four hours late! A passer-by thought 'perhaps' their destination might be over a hill, through a stream and over another hill. If it were, then they would see a big house with a white roof and would hear Christians singing.

Pastor Duma recalled, 'It was 3.00 p.m. when we finally got there and were warmly welcomed. I deferred the suggestion of a meal until after the service. The sight of a crowd of non-believers waiting for the service dispersed all weariness. Many were converted that afternoon. One was a beautiful girl with the carriage of a princess, who wept bitterly at the altar. She abandoned herself to the Lord and was immediately able to confess her salvation. Her name was Intombizethu [our girl]. On Monday a service was attended by scores of employees from a neighbouring sugar estate. Tuesday my feet were too sore from our long trek to do much walking. It was well it was so.'

As soon as Intombizethu was converted, she found herself thrown into a serious problem. She was engaged to be married, but the parents of her betrothed were both witch-doctors. The thought of marriage to him was now intolerable to her. He had, according to custom, already paid half of her bridal price, six cattle, which were in her parents' cattle kraal. The payment signified that they were engaged and that he was entitled to certain privileges. The girl, with astonishing spiritual sensitivity, asked her man where she was to be married since she was now a Christian. In her mind's eye she saw how the wedding celebrations would easily degenerate into a drunken orgy. Her ultimatum to her betrothed was, 'I am going to live a clean life. If you want to marry me you must follow my way. I must stand for Jesus Christ. You will not come to touch me before marriage, I am not your wife.'

Wrath exploded. Her parents complained, 'We are not prepared to lose the cattle for your nonsense.' Her betrothed raged, 'If you want to be a Christian you push me out. I will not have you as my wife.'

'Our Girl' remained impervious to the persuasions and prophecies of disaster to alter her decision to be a Christian and reject marriage with an ungodly man. The enraged lover demanded the immediate return of the cattle. Traditionally, it was incumbent upon the father, personally, to return the pledge of engagement. This he stubbornly refused to do. Against custom, in the bitterness of his heart, he ordered his recalcitrant daughter to herd the cattle to their old home. With a stick she leisurely drove the beasts one by one out of the cattle kraal, through the household kraal onto the path, singing with joy as she went.

It was the fashion for a betrothed girl to wear her skin or cloth skirt at a certain length below the knee and to arrange her hair in a distinctive hairstyle. Driving the cattle into her former fiancé's kraal, 'Our Girl', with magnificent dignity, twisted the skirt with a flourish to above her knee. Her hair was in a mess. It was a wordless way of saying, 'It's over.'

Her return was greeted by her father with, 'This is the last day you remain here. We will have no more of you.' She was thrown out of the home for the sake of her living Lord. In distress she remembered her Christian grandmother. They used to sit together on a mat near the fire on the hut floor at night while Granny told her stories of Jesus, long forgotten, but now flooding back into her memory. Travelling many miles to her home, she at last found her hut and was met with Granny's tears of welcome. Intombizethu found work at a store and sent money home to her parents regularly. She became the wife of a widower, an evangelist of the American Board Mission. Her parents later had a change of heart when they saw how badly their former proposed son-in-law treated his two wives.

Each Good Friday, Intombizethu tried to visit Duma at his church. 'When I see her,' he said, 'there comes back to me the trudging journey with Jali; the hunger, thirst, sore feet; the teasing aroma of the roast beef we never had – but best of all her amazing stand when she turned to Jesus.'

✛  ✛  ✛

## Govender

'Have you ever spoken to this Indian taxi driver about his soul?' The voice of the Lord broke into Duma's silent reminiscing as he made the return journey by taxi from Umkomaas, the childhood home which was still so dear to him. He was overcome with shame as he faltered, 'No, Lord, I never have.'

'You have travelled with this kind man for nine years and never once spoken to him of the Lord who loves him and died for him?'

He looked at his dear driver, Govender. Over nine years he had transported him, regardless of whether he could pay his fare or not. Often he had said, 'Govender, my friend, today I have no money. When I return on Monday I still will not be able to pay, but the next time I come I will pay all my debt.'

The gracious Indian always replied, 'My friend, you mustn't worry, some day, any day will do, but don't worry.'

The Lord had suddenly exposed his failure, balancing it against the kindness of the driver who did not know Him. 'Lord,' he whispered, 'the car is full now, I can't speak, but on Monday, with your mercy, I will say what the Holy Spirit will tell me to say.'

For the rest of the week he could not forget the Lord's rebuke and on Sunday he felt compelled to confess his failure to his flock at Umgeni Road. They were shocked that he should be so disturbed about that kind of omission. They, as he knew, were rallying excuses in their minds for him as well as for themselves.

Monday morning the taxi was empty. 'Lord, I must speak now, but I'm afraid it will break our friendship – no more lifts, but I'll take my opportunity now.'

'Govender, what sort of people do you carry in this bus?'

'Oh, Pastor, all sorts – teachers, ministers, working men and women...'

'How many do you carry?'

'On Saturday always full, the capacity is from fifteen to thirty.'

'My friend, I want to ask you another question. Has anyone ever spoken to you about Jesus?'

'No.'

'Dear friend, I know you are not a Christian. I am going to say something which might offend you, but please, nothing must break our friendship. The Lord Jesus has told me to speak, it is my duty, I must. It is my task to bring people to Jesus. I don't want you to swallow a piece of bread if you don't want it, but listen, Govender. Do you know that this car you are driving may one day be driven by someone else, perhaps by your brother? On that day, when they go to get a box, a coffin, it will be a very sad day when the flies can sit on you where they like and you can't brush them off; when you can't write a letter to your wife to say where you are. I know you worship idols, but on that day you must belong to Jesus Christ. It would be a terrible day if you died without God. I know you don't like to think about it.'

Duma recalled, 'Govender pulled to the side of the road and opened the window. I thought he was going to throw me out. He put his face through the opened window, crying, catching his breath between long, broken sobs. He said, "Let us go back and you speak to my wife. I must, I must take Jesus. My elder brother will never agree, he will throw me out. You come back with me now."

' "Friend, I cannot come back now, but next Saturday, the Lord will bring me back to see you and your wife."

'I returned as promised, with three victorious Christian black men of my church. We went to his home where he lived with his prosperous brother who owned the house, shop, taxis and buses. His brother welcomed us into his home. I said to Govender, "Tell your brother what you have decided." His wife dodged and ran away.

'Govender said, "My brother, I have decided to become a Christian."

'What an explosion! When he found that Govender was firmly determined to follow Christ, his brother said, "I'll have nothing more to do with you. You must leave here and make your own way", and he walked out of the house, furious. We went with Govender to his part of the shared house and prayed with his wife and him. Seeing idols of clay and wood around the room, I told him he must destroy them, explaining he couldn't serve Jesus Christ and retain the idols. He smashed those of clay and burnt those of wood. Because of his brother's angry opposition, he was forced to move his furniture to his small farm in the country, where he built an iron shanty and lived while still driving a taxi. He became a valiant Christian. God blessed him abundantly so that at the year's end he was able to buy more cars and to build a house. It was well known that he was a Christian. He spoke beautiful, fluent Zulu, better than I can speak it, and often ministered to my flock at Umkomaas, where he was loved. He also preached at Umgeni Road church. He made no secret of his Christianity among his own Indian community and many became Christians.'

Before leaving for the Berlin Congress on Evangelism in 1966, Duma journeyed down the coast especially to say goodbye to him. While the pastor was away there was an Indian wedding in his district. The bridal family said they could not trust drivers because they got drunk, but they knew Govender was a Christian and safe. Very reluctantly, Govender finally consented to drive a big bus on the occasion. Returning home, after the celebrations, the drunken passengers commenced a wild fight, falling over each other, quarrelling, barging into one another until they crashed into the driver's seat. They dislodged Govender and he lost his grip on the steering wheel. He couldn't gain control and the vehicle overturned killing seven, including the gentle Govender. He was deeply mourned and continuously missed.

## The Chief's Son

Magwaza, deacon of Umgeni Road Church, Durban, was the owner of a flourishing business. He lived in Zululand and it was his custom wherever he went to tell the love story of his life, the story of Jesus and himself. People often said that this man nearly forgot his business talking about his God.

Sitting outside a hut talking to a stranger, he heard that the chief was nose to the ground in sorrow. His son, heir to the chieftainship, was dangerously ill. White specialists, doctors, hospital, witchcraft – none of them could do anything.

Magwaza went to visit the chief. Admitted to the hut, he saw that he sat silent, apart from his advisors and family. Magwaza performed the traditional courtesies and offered expressions of sympathy, aware that the chief didn't hear a word he said, nor did he wish to hear. Anguish and grief were written over every face.

Suddenly, Magwaza, clothed with the authority of the Holy Spirit, his voice in a different register, began to tell the story of God's power to heal. He told of the *umfundisi* to whom the Great One had given power to heal by a special anointing of His Spirit and the bestowed power of prayer. Magwaza told story after story of healings of incurable diseases. The chief listened, silent, expressionless but for the shadows of doubt passing over his face. He slowly shook his head in disbelief. Undeterred and undaunted Magwaza told the old, old story over again. He told it simply, slowly, but the chief couldn't take it in.

Then unexpectedly, 'How do I get to this *umfundisi*?' A bed was placed in the large Kombi. The son of twenty years was carried with the gentlest care, placed on a bed to travel the many miles to Durban. In an anguish of uncertainty and pain the chief drove away from his puzzled, weeping people and from the tribal foundations of his life. Waves of indecision washed over him. 'Am I taking my son to a strange man, away from the home and customs of my ancestors, only to bring him home in a box?' But a strange power in Magwaza, sitting at his side, seemed to make turning back impossible.

Duma took up the story. 'It was our prayer meeting morning. The church was packed. There was a great commotion at the door and someone was being brought in on a bed. I told the deacons to take the man to the vestry and wondered what it was all about. The congregation was singing and their rich voices were lifted by the power of praise. In the pulpit I was caught up with such joy that I could not sing. While they sang on I went to the vestry. I tried to raise the very ill young man to a sitting position. He collapsed and fell back on me. With the triumphant singing surging around me, I prayed a simple prayer, saturated with faith bestowed for that very moment in time and knew, beyond any shadow of a doubt, that God had healed him. With a heart full of praise I returned to the pulpit. Later, I learned that the father had been deeply disappointed at the brevity of my prayer. Had he brought his dying boy all those miles for those few words?

'After the service, I found the young man walking slowly, tentatively up and down the vestry, the first walk in many months. He spent the night with me, his father electing to use the accommodation especially provided for chiefs in a township.

' "But, *Mfundisi*, what happened?" burst from the young man's lips with awed wonder, as he looked in amazement at the legs that now walked! "But I haven't walked for months! Now look, *Mfundisi*." I smiled at him, understanding so well the glow of a divine miracle. '*Mfundisi*, what can I do for this Jesus who did this big thing for me? I've long known His Name but He seemed to be in a book, long, long ago." I tried to answer his avalanche of questions but the fact of his healing was his doorway to faith in the Divine Deliverer.

'Next morning was my market day. The young man walked all the long way with me, over a mile. He insisted on carrying the empty baskets there and the full ones on our return. The courtly old chief, when he came to take his son home, shook his head with puzzled joy on his radiant face. It was all beyond him. Sitting with his boy beside him, all he could repeat was, "The thorn is out – the worry is gone."

'We were leaving one morning later in the month for a service in a distant township. A vehicle had stopped outside the church. Bags of mealies, beans, pumpkins and much else were being unloaded, all for the poor. It was the chief and his chief *induna*. They accepted an invitation to go with us. While I was preaching the good news of the Word of God, the tall, kingly old gentleman stood up with his hand raised and clearly announced, "I want this Jesus. I want to belong to Him, I want to serve Him."

'When I get discouraged, I often hear the youth's voice, "But, *Mfundisi*, you said so few words and Jesus came quicker than a bird flies." That is it. A few words and He comes with the old amazing power and the same results.'

# Chapter 11

## Prisoners of Christ

*'I tell you the truth, today you will be with me in paradise.'*
(Luke 22:43)

New doors began to open up for Duma providing opportunities for ministry he would never have imagined. Along with ministers from other denominations he was invited to conduct services for black police trainees at Wentworth, Durban. Eventually he was asked by government officials to be responsible for all their services. He was shocked at the suggestion.

'What do you mean by that? Other ministers must have their opportunities.'

'If you do not take over, many services will be discontinued.'

'But what is wrong?'

'Wrong is not the word. Through many months senior officials, as you know, have attended each service. They have listened intently. Each preacher to a greater or lesser degree has made the focal pressure of his address, an urgent invitation to join his particular church. You, alone, of them all, have lifted up the Name of Jesus Christ as the summit of your message. Never have you thrown out a net for your church. If you cannot come with your pure message, trainees will suffer a great loss.'

Duma was distressed and for Duma distress meant isolating himself in prayer. He reported, 'The Lord told me to take up my cross. I could guess what gossip and probable jealousy would be provoked by this and I knew that it would indeed be a cross.' As time passed, many of the officers who attended these services gave their lives to God. They formed a prayer group and Duma believed that their prayers strongly undergirded his ministry as well as influencing their colleagues. In frequent travels throughout the Republic Duma came across keen Christians who remembered Wentworth as the place they met with God. Services continued under Duma until the training centre was transferred to another town.

In addition to his church duties, Duma, like many other pastors, visited those in prison. One day he received a telephone call summoning him to the Department of Justice. All the way there he was perplexed as he tried to guess what the possible reason for the summons could be, but once he knew he was overwhelmed by what he instantly recognised as God's plan. He was asked by the Government to travel by aeroplane to Pretoria to minister to prisoners awaiting the death sentence and those serving long prison terms. Impressed by the sincere concern of the authorities for the spiritual condition of these unfortunate prisoners, Duma agreed.

One of the men Duma met through the prison visits was Naidoo – a man he could never forget. Naidoo had murdered his brother following a dispute over the finance of a company in which his whole family was involved. While in prison a deeply caring Swiss missionary had led him to Christ. One day, when his family visited him, he announced that he was a Christian. He told them of his ceaseless, bitter sorrow for what he had done. He pleaded for the forgiveness which he did not deserve. They were Hindus and furious at his defection from the family religion. When, shortly before his execution, he sent a message asking them to come and say goodbye to him, they replied that, unless he forgot his nonsense of being a Christian, they preferred not to see him. Duma recalled, 'I found him one morning in agony because of his family's rejection. The sorrow for his crime was unremitting. I never doubted that spiritually he was a transformed man. The gentle, steady look in his eyes, his gracious words and gratitude could never be simulated. For what purpose would he deceive me? He could have sat silent and morose as many prisoners did.' Duma realised that, although Naidoo knew God had forgiven him at the time of his repentance, yet he had no peace.

'I'll never forget how I worked hard with him in his despairing need of peace. It was a struggle to pray. I trod with him through the deepest darkness. We spoke of the dying thief on the cross who, at the last moment, received Christ's peace and promise of immediate Paradise. Leaving him to visit other cells, my heart was so weighed down for his condition that I went back to visit him an hour later. His face lit up when he saw me again. I was determined that somehow he would receive the inheritance of Christ's healing peace. We prayed and talked. His brother arrived with the guitar he had sent for. White and black police were present – they accompany all visitors to every cell as a safety measure. He sang his favourite hymn:

> Take my life and let it be
> Consecrated, Lord, to Thee;
> Take my moments and my days
> Let them flow in ceaseless praise.

'In that cell where death beckoned, the exquisite beauty of his voice, singing, was almost unbearable. Again I implored in prayer that God's special dove of peace should touch and heal him. When I opened my eyes there was peace on his brow. I can see him now smiling through a veil of fast-flowing tears as he cried with wonder, "It is mine: oh it is mine! Peace, peace has come: it is mine."'

✛ ✛ ✛

Phillip, a young Zulu of sixteen, had returned from work one afternoon under the influence of drink. Both his parents were strongly addicted to the poisonous home-made concoction known as *isishimiyane* and another called *gavin*. They had introduced him to these strong drinks while still very young, and so it was no surprise that by the age of sixteen he was a drunk. Entering the home one day he found his mother cooking on a Primus stove. A mother and son argument arose. His mother playfully brandished a large knife before him saying, 'Phillip, I will kill you' – a common Zulu expression often used playfully rather like the English, 'I'll give you a good hiding.' In his drunken state he grabbed the knife from his mother and stabbed her three times while she screamed, 'Phillip, why are you killing me?' She died in the ambulance on her way to McCord's Mission Hospital. Through the future, unforgiving, relentless years the son could not forget her anguished cry, 'Phillip, why are you killing me?'

Duma came across young Phillip in the cells in Pretoria. His head between his knees, a pool of water at his feet, he was weeping bitterly. Duma's fatherly heart was deeply moved, he put his arms around the boy and said, 'My son, why are you weeping so?'

'Oh, my sins are so heavy on my shoulders.'

The young man told the Pastor of how his father, who later abandoned the home, took him to cinemas when he was very young. 'For years I saw films where people went wild, killing each other, shouting and howling with joy when they saw the dead. It was all made out to be wonderful. That was the school in which I learned these things. How could I even dream that one day I would do this thing to the mother I loved so much? I blame the pattern of killing which was ploughed into my mind without my knowing it was there.'

When Phillip was transferred to the Transvaal, to an institution for boys, Duma lost touch with him. One Sunday evening when he was standing at the church door shaking hands with the worshippers as they left, a young man surprised him by grabbing both his hands. He began crying aloud as if deeply upset. Duma was shocked, not knowing what it was all about. A deacon, thinking there might be trouble, ran to help. The youth said, 'My *Mfundisi*, don't you know me? Don't you remember the boy you visited in gaol who killed his mother?' Even though he had been in prison for fourteen years he was still overshadowed by the dark memory of his crime. Still standing at the door, Phillip talked on, 'My work has been in the fields on a large agricultural farm where younger criminals are detained. Now I am free.'

Phillip had come to the Pastor because he had given him a New Testament with his name and address on it. He was without friends and he had searched without success for his sister. He said, his heart torn with pain, 'This is the only place I could come to.' Duma could see he was longing for him to take him for the night. Hesitating, he told him to come back the next day.

'He came – so joyously pleased to be with me. While he told me the story of those fourteen years, he didn't know he was reading to me a journal of a heart's deep agony and ceaseless grief. Although he had only a grain of knowledge of what his "adoption" into the family of God meant, that grain had kept him going, preventing his spiritual collapse when the dark wheel of memory ground him down to the past. There were very evil youths in gaol. There was little to help him in the church services. "It is then, *Mfundisi*, I remembered how you taught me to pray. I nursed the memory of that hour in the prison when you first took me by the hand to Jesus. You prayed as though Jesus was alive in that cell. That helped me to struggle through a thick bush of thorns. When my mother's face came before me as she cried, 'Phillip, why are you killing me?' your words came back to me, *'If we confess our sins, He is faithful and just and will forgive us our sins and purify us from all unright-eousness'* (1 John 1:9). I wonder if anyone, anywhere, ever kept repeating those words to himself as I did."'

Duma prayed with him and tried to show him love. Ultimately Phillip found his auntie and lived with her while working as a casual labourer. He was encouraged to spend each weekend with the Dumas. The companionship of the

Duma boys was a great pleasure which never failed to bring laughter to his face and contentment to his eyes. But between midnight and 2.00 a.m. anguished screaming would come from his bedroom. He would be found sitting in a chair moaning, 'I see my mother. I hear her crying, "Why do you do this, Phillip?"'

At his request he was baptised. He had a rich, rare singing voice and played a guitar with skill. He loved being part of a quartet for church services. But suddenly, like the swooping of a bird upon its prey, dark memories seized his mind, bringing him into deep confusion.

Duma recalled, 'Scenes of his murder returned ever more frequently – intervals of calm were less and less. There came a period in a mental institution. After apparent recovery he came to us, only to return for further treatment. After an unusually long absence we learned he had disappeared. Enquiries failed to trace him. We never saw him again. The alcohol given to Phillip in his tender years wrecked his whole system including his brain.'

At that time the Durban Municipal Health Authorities were deeply concerned about the effects of the brews referred to by the Zulus as 'concoctions'. It was discovered that carbide and other noxious agents were used as ingredients. Despite extensive campaigns by the municipal health authorities to try to explain the disastrous health hazards and stamp the trade out, it was a losing battle. It was too profitable. Phillip was just one of innumerable victims whose lives were ruined.

Xhoso was a teacher by profession with a BA degree. As he sat in the prison chapel, his elbows on his knees, his eyes weary with weeping, his heart was torn by Pastor Duma's words as he preached from Proverbs, *'If a man digs a pit he will fall into it; if a man rolls a stone, it will roll back on him'* (Proverbs 26:27). The Holy Spirit was there in tremendous power. The Sergeant-in-charge spoke to the man, but he neither moved nor answered. Putting his hand on the prisoner's shoulder and bending to comfort him, Duma whispered, 'What can I do for you?' His words were scarcely audible through his sobs, 'My sin weighs heavy on my shoulders.' The Sergeant said softly, 'It is a big trouble.'

In a rich and beautifully enunciated English, Xhoso told the story of how he had taught in a school in the Transkei and had fallen in love with a girl under age who had become pregnant. She died at the birth of the child. He was tried, imprisoned and transferred to Durban. He lived hourly with the dastardly deed perpetrated against the young girl and faced the bleak long road of the eighteen years which was his sentence. He was the arrogant thief who had robbed her young beauty of the right to live. The memory tortured him day and night. The vision of her trusting, innocent young face never left him. As Duma preached, Xhoso began to grasp the promise of forgiveness at the cross offered to him now. That day, by the grace of God, he was able to accept the incredible fact that forgiveness was his. When next the pastor visited him Xhoso told him that, although there were still times when memory of the past haunted him, his life was changed.

He was gripped with an intense longing for people to hear the story of his redemption. The deacons at Umgeni Road prayed much for him. They decided to go to a Baptist lawyer friend, the late W.T. Clarke and to a Baptist retired magistrate, Mr Reimer, to ask the local gaol officials to approach Pretoria to allow him to attend church. On a specific Sunday he was granted leave for three hours. The day before, Duma went to market, bought chickens, meat and all the things he might like to taste to make the day more special. The meal was before the afternoon service. As they began to eat he took a little food, then, putting down his knife and fork he said, 'It is hard to eat this food in such company.' The food reminded him of a much loved mother. 'I can't help thinking of my return to fifteen more years in prison. Do not think the food is not very delicious. I can't eat for sorrow.'

The church was crowded with young people, Blacks, Indians, Coloureds and a few Whites. Pastor Duma opened the service, then handed it over to him to speak. He began to tell the story of what had happened before he was convicted. The whole church was in tears. There was such tremendous sympathy, love and sorrow for the man who had found Christ and had been forgiven. His confession brought other confessions that afternoon. Many came forward in deep awareness of their sins and wanting to repent.

Because of the indescribable 'something' about him since his conversion, he was given a special duty as secretary-in-charge of visitors. He became an evangelist within the prison, telling his story to his fellow inmates and asking for Bibles in their own language for distribution. These were supplied by white friends.

At the end of fifteen long years, at Christmas, he received the gift of discharge for exemplary and Christian service – three years commuted. After two years in the Umtata district, the government gave him a responsible post connected with the court. Zealous for the Lord, he had in his heart a burning passion to proclaim the love of God. He received a call from God to go to Fort Hare to prepare for the ministry. When he applied, there was a division among the officials as to whether a man 'with such a past' should be accepted. Finally they refused his application. Bowed with disappointment he wrote to Duma, who took up his cause. 'I said to myself, "I will fight and fight to the end till this man with such a testimony and power of the Holy Spirit is accepted." I wrote under the authority of the Holy Spirit. I asked, "Do you want angels for ministers, or a man who is washed in the blood of the Lamb of God, a man severely tested for fifteen difficult years and triumphant through Christ? I am the man who has sweated and wept and prayed through the weary years with him."'

Finally Xhoso was accepted, went to college and became a minister of a well-known denomination whose favourite theme was always the unearned mercy of God to the sinner.

✢ ✢ ✢

Fifteen African men killed by one of their own race with an axe! The story hit the headlines and the notorious criminal became known as the 'Axe Killer'. Brought to judgement, he stubbornly contended that his crime was committed on the instruction of Tokoloshe. Who is Tokoloshe? A legendary dwarf who lives near rivers amongst boulders and in reeds. Only children may see him – after puberty they lose the ability. The authorities were not prepared to accept such a reason for the crime and medical specialists who examined the prisoner concluded that there was no mental derangement. Chiefs of various tribes were authorised by the government to visit him in the Pretoria prison in an effort to elicit the hidden reason for his infamous crime. It was most unlikely the chiefs would deny the existence of the dwarf, but they might smell out a contributory factor causing the massacre. The prison chaplain and a Swiss missionary visited Msome and were totally ignored. His face was hard as granite.

It was with a heart full of trepidation and much prayer that Duma entered the notorious cell which he described as 'stepping into a cauldron of hell.' Recalling the experience he said, 'I see him now. The coat of his suit neatly belted, he stood, shaking and twirling his body from left to right and vice versa with the same jigging of shoulders and torso which certain dancers affect. It was a macabre scene intensified by the unblinking mockery of his eyes. He returned an arrogant silence at the suggestion of prayer and was totally oblivious of his sin. The only words he spoke as I left were, "I do not want those chiefs to come. I will see them in hell and not before." There followed me down the passage in a loud voice the scalding words, "I will see them in hell." Later I learned that the axe killer was a witchdoctor in league with Tokoloshe. Having involved himself with the Dwarf, it was impossible, without the help of Almighty God, to disentangle himself from the power of Satan.'

It was not the first time that Pastor Duma had come across Tokoloshe. His first engagement with him had been in the house of the widow Shozi, one of the saints at

Umkomaas. She had lost five children and one by one he had buried them in separate graves. He had asked her 'Mama Shozi, what will you do now? You are like Naomi.'

She replied, 'The Lord has examined the death of the family. He saw the burden was heavy. I can now manage the problems of family. I will be stronger in the Lord.' Raising her hand she said, 'Today I am victor in Christ's power.'

Into the wonderful faith of this home trouble entered. During the night two daughters screamed in agonising fear. Something under the bed was shaking the mattress violently so that the occupants were tossed up and down. Shozi asked neighbours what it could be. Unanimously they said, 'It is the sign of Tokoloshe who uses quickly tapping feet so that everything he touches is thrown about.'

It was reported that in the district a pair of oxen ploughing the field suddenly stampeded – the yokes were invisibly tampered with and the oxen scattered. The farmers fled home, terrified by the disruption of their quiet routine. In huts where families were eating their *amasi*, food was rapidly snatched away by an invisible power. 'Tokoloshe', Duma explained, 'is one of the vast desecrating company known as *Umthakathi* (those who have devilish powers of bewitchment) – *Umthakathi* is one of the devil's own brigades. Tokoloshe frequently uses baboons as his agents.' In the midst of this evil invasion he prayed and fasted for two days. He continued the story:

'Deacon Jali and I were in the home of the distraught Shozi family. As it was getting dark he saw a frightened child run to his mother screaming and clutching her crying, "I've seen a boy." Immediately, a stench filled all nostrils and contaminated clothing. We all froze with fright. Jali put his foot under my leg as if for protection and pressed his chair close to mine for comfort and safety. I suffered the intense torture of a threatening disaster which I could neither diagnose nor dodge. Loudly I called, "Let us pray." I said three words only, "In Jesus' Name". Immediately something undiscernible and indescribable passed by my

chair. I heard the feeling (felt the rhythm) of flying footsteps and of vibrant breathing. I rushed outside, heard a
wild running around and I followed. By that time I was a
changed person. I was empowered by the anointing of the
Holy Spirit as I fled after the unseen runner. He ran with far
greater agility than I could. I followed him down a narrow
path which ended in a steep decline to the river. I had no
fear, I was in a state of exaltation. The runner arrived at the
river ahead of me and I heard an explosive splash of water as
though a huge boulder had been thrown in. I then vividly
understood what had happened. The holy anointing which
I had received in that dramatic slice of time was lifted. With
the removal of power a veil was also removed and with their
absence I re-inherited the human weakness of fear. I knew
Satan was on guard at that river. It was eerily quiet down
there. I shouted to the people who had followed me, "I'm
here." I was frightened the Thing would come back.

'I was a young Pastor and shouted, "Come, take me
home", as a little child might call. Every vestige of my
clothing was impregnated with the stench which had come
from the diabolical visitor. I was loaned a suit while my
clothing was washed. I awoke the next morning with a great
uneasiness, as if I were fighting an enormous black cloud. I
fasted and prayed for a full day to rebuke the uneasiness
which lingered. I recovered the peace of God and the
intimacy of God's Fatherhood to the child in me. While
under the Holy Spirit's anointing, I am often, as it were, out
of the body, not acutely aware, for instance, of what a
person looks like for whom I am interceding for healing. I
move, have my being, do things which are not of my
mental contriving. When the anointing is lifted I am
surprised by accounts of the methods I use for handling
cases of healing, or of exorcism. It might be asked, "Is there
not danger in this unawareness?" Emphatically – Never!
Because I have fasted and prayed. God's answer is an
anointing and its withdrawal is sheathed in His protective
loving care for me, "the little one" of His flock.'

## Chapter 12

# Making Friends with Worldly Wealth

*'Use worldly wealth to gain friends for yourself, so that when it is gone, you will be welcomed into eternal dwellings.'*
(Luke 16:9)

William Duma became gripped with a new intention of the soul. His daily prayer became, 'Lord, I want businessmen in my church! Give me men with money: if only one man, just one, please do not withhold.' This was a very strange, out of character, request for a man who was notably unimpressed by money or material possessions. Duma explained, 'I have visited other churches with cars outside which seem to me to add "dignity"! Their people were able to support the cause of Christ. I looked at my church full of those who worked in lowly occupations. We were poor, we could do little in outreach or expansion, so I cried, "If only one businessman, Lord, I covet him for Your work in Umgeni Road."'

The first launch into the business world was made by twenty-five men who pooled their resources to open the first Christian businessmen's shop. It was run by Magwaza, a church deacon with a warm personality, and Richard Zungu, a young man with an undeniable flair for business. They were prospering and rejoicing until the bank failed and all their savings were lost. Magwaza found work in a factory. Having lost faith in banks, he insisted that his pastor should look after his savings. The day came when Duma said, 'Magwaza, I have R200 (£100) of yours. I can't keep this, it is not registered and if I died you might lose it all. You must now start another business, you have enough money.' Magwaza was distressed at the suggestion but, after prayer, decided to go ahead. A few months later he reported, 'It is not moving.' Richard Zungu was persuaded to join his staff and business began to flourish. The well-run shop with its courteous and efficient owners became the talk of the neighbourhood.

The two men worked day and night until others, envious of their success, attempted to emulate their efforts, but with little reward. Apart from their business acumen, Duma's men followed the leadings of their God in all they did. Duma insisted that no shop would be opened for the first time nor should an item be sold, until the building had been consecrated to God with a service outside. After the doors were officially opened a brief service was held inside. With childlike delight Duma said, 'Magwaza was the first bird in my business cage.' Magwaza was very successful and was a great witness in the community as people began to sense what it meant to be a Christian shopkeeper.

Mr Nxele, a member of the clerical staff of McCord's Zulu Hospital, met and married a staff nurse. Her people were in business and gave them the option of a shop in Zululand. Its opening followed the pattern established by Duma. On all such occasions the Scriptures read were Genesis 17:1–2, *'The Lord said, "I am God Almighty; walk before me and be blameless. I will confirm my covenant between me and you and will greatly increase your numbers"'*, and Genesis 12:3, *'I will bless those that bless you and whoever curses you I will curse.'*

The business soon became so prosperous that it was necessary to have a fleet of vehicles. Duma rejoiced in the success of the 'second bird in his business cage'. Nxele became, as his Pastor prayed his men should be, a missionary among his customers, his neighbours and his servants.

All was flourishing with Nxele when Duma had a vision in the night. Early in his disciplined prayer life he had been schooled not to ignore his personal visions. It was a warning that Nxele was in danger. Pastor saw 'a big black bird and lightning striking Nxele's house' and knew they were signs of impending evil. Certain that Nxele was in danger, he drove through the darkness very early in the morning to Zululand to pray with Nxele, committing him to the protection of God before returning to Durban.

A few days later, a wild, angry Black with a revolver in his hand entered the crowded shop demanding loudly, 'Where is that dog Nxele? I am going to shoot him this very day. If you don't tell me where he is I will...' He was one of a notorious gang for whom the police were hunting. Having heard that a policeman had been seen in the shop he presumed that Nxele had reported him. The terror-stricken staff said they really didn't know where he was. He must be out in one of the cars and, as many cars were out, they did not know which he had taken. No, he wasn't in the house. Long ago he had gone for breakfast and he never, never took longer than ten minutes. He had not returned, he must be away.

It was Nxele's custom to take his breakfast snack standing and to hurry back to assist serving the early morning shoppers who had walked miles and liked to get back home as quickly as possible. On that eventful morning, contrary to custom, he had a strange compulsion to indulge himself by taking breakfast sitting at a table and to linger over it. Immensely enjoying the leisurely moment, he decided to complete the novelty by resting in a comfortable chair for a quiet read.

When finally he returned to the shop, he was met with a clamour of voices, all telling the story of the revolver man. Stunned, he stood, silent, thinking of the black bird, the lightning flash and the man of God who had driven through the darkness to pray for his divine protection. He pondered the magnificent deliverance he had had, through the never-to-be-forgotten providence of God's love. The 'second bird' in the Pastor's cage was safe!

The third bird in Pastor Duma's cage was Emmanuel Zungu, younger brother of Richard, a man of impressive physique, modest, lovable, with an outgoing heart, who later became church secretary. When newly married at twenty-six with his first shop in its infancy, he became very ill with diabetes, was hospitalised only to be discharged with an open letter to his local doctor which read, 'Nothing can be done, incurable.' Emmanuel felt within himself that he was a dying man.

His brother Richard took up the story, 'Nxele and I literally carried him to Pastor. We knew his life hung on God answering prayer; his face was haggard and stamped with death. Pastor prayed for and anointed him. He was divinely, marvellously healed and journeyed back from the grave to robust health. For Emmanuel life was never the same again. He began to walk a daily pilgrimage with God in faith and prayer which was marked with a deep awareness of the unseen presence of God.'

Emmanuel was a man with an amazing business acumen. By 1975 he was operating three shops, which he had built himself. His friend Nxele and he built a church in a needy area costing R12,000. Emmanuel never sowed sparingly, nor did he reap sparingly, and God rewarded him richly. Supported by his wife in all he did, his generosity spilled over into many people's lives, in particular those of the many foster children whom he educated and, if promising, saw through university.

Richard Zungu said of the 'fourth bird of the cage','He was an eagle'. Mr Johannes X was a genius, his business seemed to grow in a week. With no learning, he romped to success and prestige. He operated two teashops, government property, each one on a railway station in a Durban township. His turnover quickly reached R1000 per day. His success was fabulous, the scale of his operation impressive by any standards. When the Minister of Transport visited the area accompanied by an official retinue, he never failed to call in, so fascinated was he by his rapid success.

X worshipped at Pastor Duma's church and was a humble, committed man who was motivated by his love for the Lord Jesus Christ in all he did, giving generously to the poor and to the church.

Pastor Duma described how Deacon Magwaza and Mr X visited him one day.

'Mfundisi, your feet have walked very wearily for a very long time over the ungracious miles of Natal. It is time you had other transport,' they said.

'They took me to a garage, paid cash and presented me with a beauty of a car. When, for big occasions, I ordered large amounts of food, X would never accept payment.

'Throughout the congregations under me, X was greatly loved, but was never spoiled nor lost the humility which endeared him so much to us all.'

Then a day came when Duma began to feel very troubled in his spirit and concerned about X. He telephoned Nxele urgently to inquire if anything was wrong. A shocked Nxele reported that X had told him to mind his own business. They both had been as close as brothers, but X had suddenly become proud, very proud, and was furious at Nxele's inquiry.

'I "smelt" Satan in great power round Mr X. I had a dream in which I saw him in tattered clothing, old socks showing through broken shoes, feet through the shoes to the ground. In agony I questioned, "What is going on?"

'At 4.00 a.m., before sunrise, I got into my car and went to X in Zululand. I was received with icy coldness. I pleaded with him to share his trouble with me. He maintained a heavy, stony silence, and my heart almost broke knowing that somewhere he had grievously disobeyed God. While silently praying, there appeared at the door a strange woman, who, discovering I was there, swiftly disappeared. Then I knew to what depths he had fallen for he was a married man. Living in adultery, his sin had isolated him from God and us, as sin always isolates. It was now obvious why he had insulted church members and friends who had visited him and why his heart was closed to God and to me. He spurned the request to pray. In anguish I said, "Dear X, I can do no more. If you will not repent, I wash my hands of you. I shall never cease to pray for your return to God and always will be waiting to welcome you." '

The woman schemed to get his money, then misused it until he was bankrupt. He tried, but could not get another shop – banks would not help. From then on he lived on his wits, a degraded pitiful figure, suffering from the fatal disease of no desire for God nor repentance – no desire to return and receive God's mercy.

That is until 1976. It was Good Friday and the church and large tent at Lamontville, the daughter church of Umgeni Road, were packed to capacity including the aisles. The Rev. A. Spann was the preacher. As worship proceeded, the Holy Spirit moved through the church and tent convicting hearts and bringing to repentance. As Pastor Spann concluded his address, Duma took his place in the pulpit, scanning the worshippers. He gave an altar call, 'You who are outside the Kingdom of God – come. Come, backslider, the Father is awaiting your return with a longing heart.'

At the word 'backslider', there arose, above the clatter of chairs, a groan which broke into deep racking sobs. Duma's eyes searched the crowded church to identify the man. They alighted upon a shabby but clean man, beard unkempt, moustache untrimmed. His heart leaped. With a jump he left the pulpit, squeezed and pushed his way through blocked aisles till he reached the weeping man. Putting his arm around the shoulder of X he said, 'Johannes, what do you want the Lord to do for you? Do you realise where you are standing today?'

Twenty-one years without communication and now here he was, kneeling before the Lord! Johannes could not stem the flood of tears as he expressed his sincere desire to return to the Lord and give himself totally back to Him. Still embracing him Duma turned to the congregation, 'Many of you do not know this dear man for whom I have prayed, without ceasing, for twenty-one long years. This is he who, with Deacon Magwaza, bought my first car because they felt walking miles was making me overtired. This is the man who gave so generously to God's cause.' As Duma spoke, a hush fell over the church. While the ageing Pastor spoke the broken man quietly wept, his wife beside him stifling her sobs.

He returned many miles to Lamontville for the Easter Sunday service. He appealed to Christians to support him in prayer, knowing he had a hard climb ahead of him. When he was asked whatever made him come to Lamont, he replied, 'I heard you were going to have a Good Friday service here. My wife urged me to come. I said, "How can I go like this? I've nothing to wear, only this ragged suit." She answered, "Those people are not looking for a smart suit, they want your heart."' The Pastor's prayer had reached the throne of God.

The young man, Richard Zungu, was for many years frustrated in his attempts to join the ranks of Pastor Duma's businessmen. As manager of a large factory's catering unit and later, sales manager of a White-owned African shop, he was highly successful while dreaming of the day he would stand behind his own counter. One day, despairing that his dream would ever be fulfilled, he went to see Pastor Duma. '*Baba*, I'm bursting to have my own shop, please help me.'

Although the Pastor agreed to join him in praying for it, he confessed, 'My heart was not in it. I couldn't pray what he asked. I cried to God, "What can I do? I've no young man to fill Richard's place, to take the responsibility of the church when, at Your call, I go all over the Republic, Rhodesia, Congo and beyond to do your bidding!"'

During the long years while he waited for his dream to be fulfilled, Richard trained and qualified as a Senior Lecturer in Health Education, as a film commentator, visual aid demonstrator, and a voice over the SABC network of Natal

and Transvaal on health subjects. He learned to grapple
with himself and his public – a profitable exercise! Three
years before his eventual 'release' from the Health Service,
Pastor Duma suggested they go to have a look at a shop for
sale in Zululand previously owned by Whites. They went,
but Zungu disliked it.

At the end of three years, Duma was praying, 'Lord, you
have blessed me with businessmen in the church, my need
is filled, Zungu can go.' He took Zungu to have another look
at the same shop which was once again for sale. This time
he liked it still less! Zungu explained, 'I had insufficient
capital. The local Blacks asked how I could succeed in a job
where the Whites had failed. They jeered, "Why don't you
eat those mouldy sweets in the bottle?" – remnants of the
former owner's stock.'

Nevertheless, 'I went to the Bantu Affairs Commission
and they gave me all I asked for! They must have liked the
look of my face! I bought the shop. My late wife and I
worked and prayed, worked and prayed with faith high. The
people mocked. They stood back watching us, repeating,
"Why have they come?" I was deeply discouraged.

'But by the end of the second year, we extended the
premises. People in trouble came for help. I noticed they
had to walk miles to get to a hospital, there being no bus
services. One day I was asked to take a very ill woman on my
own lorry to the hospital miles away. When I arrived she
was dead on the lorry! Constantly the people brought their
sick for me to take to a doctor. I couldn't refuse, neither
could I spare the time. I approached the relevant authorities
to establish a clinic in the district, which they did. Pastor
Duma's teaching of helping all in trouble wouldn't let me
go. I saw people passing wearily by, from a station miles
away. I knew that buses must be provided, but I prayed very
fervently that buses should not be my job. I knew the
endless trouble they were. I prayed, "Lord, please do not
give me that bus business."' His answer? By 1975 Richard
had six vehicles which caused him a lot of trouble because
they were always breaking down!

One day, with his spiritual sensitivity, Pastor Duma felt that something was very wrong for Zungu and telephoned to say, 'I'm burdened for you, what is wrong? I'm praying for you, I feel your trouble here at Umgeni Road.'

'Pray on, Mfundisi, I'm losing thousands of rand, pray on.' Prayers were answered, the business recovered.

Commercial travellers often asked Pastor Duma's businessmen, 'What have you Baptists got? You are all so prosperous. Shopkeepers are asking us what the secret is.' They would reply, 'There is no secret. We all talk the same language. We all belong to Christ. We are a united Christian society. We meet four times yearly in Durban for prayer and thanksgiving. Businessmen come from Swaziland, Transvaal and Natal to attend our retreats under the "Angel of the shops of the Christian – our Pastor!" Christian doctors and other professional men have been admitted to the "shop circle" at their request. White businessmen also join this unique community of praying men.'

Many people who wanted to be successful in business would approach Pastor Duma with a view to joining the association. He would always ask them one question, 'Are you saved, do you belong to Christ?' If the answer was 'no' he would always refuse their request, explaining the reason why. 'Christ is first in all our affairs, we cannot have a member who does not belong to Him. In any case, you would be extremely uncomfortable in our midst.'

For Duma two principles were key to business success. He never ceased to urge the businessmen to, *'Seek first the Kingdom of God and His righteousness and all these things shall be added unto you'* (Matthew 6:33). To this he added the all-prevailing word 'faith'.

# Chapter 13

# The Witchdoctor

Pastor Duma had received a call to visit an African woman in the country, suffering from diabetes with a gangrenous leg. With him that day was a Baptist minister, the Rev. Mr Mason in whose church in the Cape he had campaigned. They had visited the sick together and had witnessed healings and conversions. Mr Mason was shortly to return overseas and, visiting Durban, had begged Duma to take him to a Zulu witchdoctor to obtain a photo and a story. Having prayed with the sick woman, they drove inland to a famous witchdoctor.

In impeccable English, the witchdoctor said to Mr Mason, 'I want 10c (1 shilling) to speak to you.' It was paid. To the Pastor he said, 'I can't speak to both of you unless this Zulu gives me 25c.' Duma inquired to whom the money would be given. With arrogant insolence he replied, 'To the ancestors.'

Duma declared, 'I will never give for them.' To his dismay, the Rev. Mr Mason paid the devil's price on his account.

The witchdoctor sat, a middle-aged man on a low stool, skins around his shoulders and falling far down his back. He threw the coins high into the air three times incanting, *'Talani, Talani, Talani'* (thank you). At each throw the scarcely veiled antagonism on his face grew more and more threatening. He said loudly, 'My kings [evil spirits] told me you were coming. Long ago they called me from teaching in a high school to teach and work for them. I don't throw bones, that is rubbish.' With a strong, swift sweeping of his arm, indicating four walls, he commanded, 'Listen! Now that you have come they are singing. Don't you hear the singing of my kings all around the room?'

The pastors sat in appalled silence. Reverberating around the room, there was the sound of hissing as if they were surrounded by hundreds of snakes. Pastor related, 'I sat paralysed with fear, my face frozen, my mouth dry, my pulse racing. I was no longer myself. The eyes of the sorcerer were as red as the coals of the fire, scorching, darting here and there. I had to look away from his hypnotic and demonic spell. Occasionally he sipped a potion from a small container. I felt as if devilish power was trying to take me over. From the roof were suspended bottles and bags of potions and animal fats. All round the walls were the insignia of his calling – skins of snakes, birds and beasts. Mr Mason and I experienced in that hut the corrupting, destroying effects of the outskirts of hell. Terrified, I said we should make a getaway.

'I stood up and said, "Let us have prayer before we go." We could tell, from the wizard's reaction to that, that he could cheerfully have murdered us.

'The atmosphere of hell seemed to follow us to the car. As soon as we got in we both said, "Let us pray".

'Reaching home, I felt a strange, total detachment from life. I was no longer moored to anyone or anything. I felt vaguely ill, but with no definite symptom. I struggled to pray but could not. I was completely dominated by satanic fear and could not find any relief. I sent for a young minister to pray for me. I went to bed bordering on a state of being lost in utter darkness. Waking, I saw it was 1.00 a.m.

'Completely unaware of my movements, I opened the front door and followed two or three people who, in my mind, were calling to me to follow them. They walked ahead of me. From my manse to the sea would take about ten minutes' brisk walking. I didn't know I was following those people down that road and was surprised to notice the sweet smell of the sea. Those ahead of me enticed me on and on. Then a strong urging voice from the sea called three times, "Come, come, come." I went and felt the cool water round my ankles. Walking deeper into the sea, someone I did not see took hold of me, turned me to face where I had come from and shook me powerfully by taking hold of my arms. The unknown and unseen led me out of the sea and set me toward home, up the straight street I had gone down. But I was lost. I did not recognise the neighbourhood I had lived in for years. Dazed and dizzy I found myself at the Stamford Hill Railway Station, not at my home. I clambered down to the railway lines and walked between them with torn feet. I had not put shoes on when I left home. I was clothed in pyjamas and a dressing gown. My overwhelming longing was to die. I kept saying, "If only a train would come so that I could lie down and die." Then memory partially returned and I realised that my dear brother lived near that station. I went to him and he took me home. It was after 2.00 a.m. The door was still open as I had left it. For two days I continued to feel dizzy and surrounded by the deepest darkness.

'Then I went to dear precious Emolweni, where God had anointed me for my ministry. I arrived in a state of confusion. The first day I struggled against the darkness of my soul. My spirit was crushed within me, I couldn't pray. Then I lay face downwards on the blessed earth. By the end of the second day I began to revive, to sense the dear Presence I loved. The gloom was pierced with a flickering light. Faith, that dear gift and companion of my days, returned. By nightfall my heart was warmed and restored.'

Pastor Duma explained why, when in the past he had dealt with scores of people often possessed by violent evil spirits, he had suffered such devastating consequences from his encounter with the witchdoctor. 'When dealing with the demonic, I have always claimed the protection of the Atoning Blood of Jesus Christ. I always think that the Blood is on the lintel of my heart as it was on the lintels and the doorposts when the angel of death passed over the blood-sprinkled homes of the Jews long ago in Egypt. But the morning I had unexpectedly been asked to take Mr Mason to a witchdoctor, I had not prepared myself in prayer. I was vulnerable, I was off guard and walked into the situation unknowingly. The witchdoctor had given himself totally to Satan and was one of his super powerful agents. The visit was to have been for a momentary snapshot with which the Rev. Mr Mason would illustrate his story . . . that was all . . . so I thought. But there is a compensation. It seemed to me I had been to a training school on demons and evil spirits. I knew, as never before, how to warn people against dabbling with the occult. If they did, unless delivered by the power of the Holy Spirit, their end would surely be spiritual death and physical deterioration.'

As to the man in the sea, for Pastor Duma there was no doubt whatsoever that he was one of whom Dr Billy Graham writes in his book, *Angels: God's Secret Agents*, and the three who beckoned him down to the sea were clearly ambassadors of Satan.

Every true believer in Christ should be encouraged and strengthened. Angels are watching. They mark your path. They superintend the events of your life and protect the interest of the Lord God, always working to promote His plans and to bring about His Highest will for you. Angels are interested spectators and mark all you do, for *'We have been made a spectacle to the whole universe, to angels as well as to men'* (1 Corinthians 4:9). God assigns angelic powers to watch over you.

# Chapter 14

# A Healer Healed

In April 1973 the following article appeared in *The South African Baptist*:

I [William Duma] crave permission from the Editor to share with friends who prayed for me during my recent illness, the story of the glory and the grace with which God sustained me.

It was my twelfth day in hospital. I was no better, sorely puzzled and asked the specialist to discharge me. He was outraged at the request. I explained I was a man of faith and felt that God was leading me to the country to drink my own medicine by seeking His healing as I had sought for others for thirty-four years. The specialist consented. I went to Zululand believing that God was calling me into a deeper relationship with Him.

My hostess was a Christian black nurse. Through the days she watched as gusts of pain bore down as wheat bows before a hurricane. Then followed periods in which I sought, in the darkness of my tunnel, the light of His will. Came the hour when God said to me, 'Go back to your church, I'll speak to you there.'

Returning, I requested that a bed on which I could lie should be placed over against the Communion Table. There I remained from 7.00 p.m. until 3.00 a.m.

What a pageant of miracles passed over me! There was a child delivered of demons. She had been sent by a German doctor with the note, 'This is a case for you, it is not within my medical scope.' I looked again into the faces of men with eyes as hard as pebbles, watched rivers of sullen tears course down their cheeks until, yielding their wills to God, radiance like a golden dawn transformed their faces. I saw again the agony in eyes of despair because of loved ones marked for death and when, answering prayer, God touched them, I witnessed joy beyond the barriers of human language.

All these and many more scenes the Lord reviewed with me. As I mused, Satan appeared in human form taunting me with, 'You have been used of God in the past, but you are forgotten now. He has no further use for you.' I rebuked him in the Name of Jesus. He disappeared and through the church there stole peace ineffable filling me with unutterable content.

That night for the first time I slept without drugs. I was renewed but not healed. Seven days I waited in prayer; then came a vision of the Lord. He opened a fold of curtain to reveal, in awful contrast, a multiracial crowd, suffering from diseases, accidents, violences. I heard singing and looking up, saw a throng, amongst which was a white deacon whom many of you know. The Lord took my hands and said, 'You are not joining that choir yet, I have work for you. Go back to Zululand, I will restore health unto you and heal you of your wounds ... go there and wait.'

Sitting on a veranda, waiting on God, looking with unseeing eyes at the road, I became aware of a white car approaching until it stopped at the foot of the steps. A white man approached with painful effort, swaying from side to side. 'I'm looking for Pastor Duma.'

'I am he.'

'I want you to pray with us. My wife is in the car; she has had an accident, both legs broken. She has had surgery but can only shuffle in pain. In the same accident our daughter was killed. In a different accident I was seriously injured. We need your prayers.'

As he recited his sorrows I grew ever more weary. 'I've been very ill,' I said. 'Can you not see I'm not recovered? I really can't pray with you today.'

He pressed his plea, 'We've come a thousand miles from Umtali to see you. The Lord sent us.'

I turned to the nurse saying in Zulu, 'What can I do? He is so persistent, he demands.'

He interrupted with, 'It is not for you to take counsel with a human. This is a matter between God and you, you must decide this.'

I retired for prayer and, returning, asked for the wife to be brought up. It seemed an eternity while she shuffled up the few steps, inch by suffering inch, with the aid of supports. What a strange little company the fingers of God had drawn together through time and space for an appointment with Him.

The atmosphere on the veranda was loaded with weariness, the only surety was a compulsion to pray. Dully I began a simple prayer when suddenly the veranda was charged with Power 'immense and free', the Divine Fifth in our presence almost visible.

The woman broke into praise, discarded her supports, walked with comparative ease and her prayer was in another tongue, most exquisite to the ear like a prelude to a heavenly aria. Her husband sobbed, prayed, loosened his spinal support and walked upright – and, how shall I tell it? He touched me, I was healed, my body vibrant with His pulsating life and under the power of the Holy Spirit my prayer also was in another tongue. Hours later I watched the car go down the road, it seemed to be moving to the sound of unseen trumpets. Then God spoke to me, 'This which has happened is because in all my dealing you have been obedient, even to this last prayer.' I little knew that before my illness a very close friend waiting on God for me and my ministry was stunned to hear the Lord say, 'Your friend Duma, I am bringing into affliction shortly!' The shocked response was, 'Have I heard aright, is it really You speaking?' The dear familiar Voice, still small, clear, replied, 'It must be so.'

Through all the mystery, pain and waiting, there was given to me grace upon sovereign grace which abundantly sufficed, for which I ceaselessly thank God.

Events leading up to this moment of miraculous divine intervention had indeed been full of mystery, pain and waiting. They had been preceded by a very black period in Duma's ministry which had begun back in the sixties.

For a long time the church had been riding high in the power of the Holy Spirit with packed services, conversions, healings, miracles. Flooded with invitations from all over the Republic and many denominations to conduct campaigns, Duma became absorbed in the preparations for his itinerary, which included addressing Bible College students, the Baptist Assembly, and coloured and black churches. It represented months of evangelism.

Duma recalled, 'Through the years, at 4.00 a.m., by appointment with my Lord, I had been fed by the Hand of God. The busyness of preparation ate into my early morning appointment with God. Less and less time was spent in deep communion with God. I told myself I was praying earnestly for the campaigns. Vaguely at first, I realised that my personal communion, consisting of listening, renewal, revelation, rebuke, guidance and much else, had tailed off. The super-abundant harvest of those early mornings with God was replaced by severe spiritual *kwashiokor*! I tried to justify myself, "Time taken up for campaigning is not only legitimate but imperative." To this my troubled conscience whispered, "Not at the perilous neglect of the sweet, fresh hours with Him at dawn." My spirit became a scorched desert. I began reading books to use what other preachers had written. I became physically tired, whereas previously the Lord had sustained and resuscitated my body and spirit through long periods of tremendous strain. I was a deteriorating man, body, soul and spirit. Being tired, I made flimsy excuses to God but even my prejudiced eyes saw my ministry was failing. Healing power was not as it was formerly. Where were the seeking souls at the altar? The high-powered action of the Holy Spirit on the work was frighteningly reduced. Shocked, I realised that a weed of pride was blossoming abundantly when I began to fear people were saying, "He's not the same man he used to be."'

It was during this period when Duma was a spiritual low that a young Zulu, who had attended Umgeni Road

Church, returned from Bible School to be ordained and assist at the township churches. The gift of discernment, so prominent in the pastor's ministry, was dormant. He did not perceive that the young man's heart was full of jealously and that he coveted the pastor's city pulpit for himself. Appointed to a township pastorate, the new minister began to spread seeds of opposition and disruption.

Some time before the young minister had arrived, a woman discharged from hospital with an incurable heart condition, attended the Prayer Circle and was permanently healed. Although a member of the township church, she attended Umgeni Road every Wednesday, proclaiming the story of her healing with the same enthusiasm as the woman of Samaria at that famous well. Her cry was, 'Go, see what God is doing at Umgeni Road.' The new young pastor objected and forbade her to worship there. Catching something of the antagonism of the pastor's jealous heart, she obeyed his edict. A church friend of hers, suffering from asthma, innocently announced that she also was going to Duma for prayer. The young pastor and his ally, the healed woman, instructed her not to go. Dominated by their threats and her own fear, she stayed away.

Duma recalled, 'Rumours of my alleged dishonesty began circulating from the pastor. He declared I would not pray "unless you pay" – that I received cash from Europeans and Indians for my prayers. Lies surrounded me. My already debilitated spirit sank into a pit of antipathy nearing hate.'

'At my church's lowest ebb, the young pastor became incurably ill with medically diagnosed elephantiasis in his leg. One morning in prayer, I distinctly heard the Lord say, "Duma, go and help that man." Although long ago now I recall with shame my response, "Lord, I will never go to help that man." The voice repeated, "Duma, go help that man." I still shrink, recalling my rebellious reply, "I will never. He has campaigned to ruin my ministry and nearly succeeded." Almost immediately, appalled by my wrong spirit, I cried in deep repentance, "Lord, please send Clifford

Nxumalo to me. I don't know where to contact him. I cannot go to that man alone."

'Clifford came. I urged him, "Clifford you must be my witness, if I go alone he will twist my words." We went. I discovered he visited witchdoctors regularly while continuing his ministry. The name of the Baptist Church was being dishonoured.

'Prior to our arrival, the *inyanga* cut his trousers, so swollen was his leg, to make an incision in which to put his quack medicine. The stench from his condition filled the room, as also did his intense hatred for me. I remonstrated with him for calling Satan to heal him instead of asking God's forgiveness and restoration. The mutiny reflected in his face was frightening. Suddenly my heart filled with anguish and pity for his condition. My visit being at the command of God, with a love born of the Holy Spirit, I gently suggested that we would like to pray for him. He would have none of it. Later he transferred to a church in Zululand where he associated with witchdoctors and *izinyanga*. Finally, taken to hospital, he could not be admitted. On the return journey in his son's car, he died.

'The healed woman who had linked with the young pastor to wreck my church was suddenly taken ill and admitted to hospital. Her constant cry was, "Bring Duma to me. I need his prayers." Her friends asked me to visit her. I replied, "Of course I will go, I am glad she sent for me." Again and again I planned that visit but repeatedly, however hard I tried, something urgent, unavoidable, impossible to put off, prevented my going. She died without my seeing her.

'At this time, congregations were increasing, but I no longer enjoyed my ministry. I missed the joy of the Lord. My old enemy Screwtape taunted me again and again with, "Hm! Hm! You had a great ministry in healing. Now all you do is to wobble. You may die without joy between your Lord and you." '

One morning, Father Francis, Chaplain of St Aidan's Indian Anglican Hospital, a faithful counsellor at Prayer

Circle, felt an unaccountable urge to visit the pastor. He found him rolling in agony, sweating profusely, unable to speak. He summoned a doctor. With Duma too dangerously ill to wait for an ambulance, they rushed him by car to St Aidan's Hospital. Three doctors, one a specialist, agreed that there was a possibility of a stroke and death. They thought he might never recover.

Close to death, in hospital and desolate, Duma read the story of Hezekiah in Isaiah 38. 'Reading of Hezekiah's reprieve I was comforted. The tears I wept and wept into my pillows cleansed my attitude toward the young pastor. I mourned like a dove in Lebanon for the resentment I had allowed to make a travesty of my ministry. I grieved for the spiritual capital which had drained away because my first eager communion with God at daybreak had been shortened, if not replaced, by campaign planning. Those recollections broke my heart and I wept into the pillows.'

Broken in spirit but restored to the Lord through repentance Duma heard God speak to him telling him to discharge himself from the hospital and there followed the glorious chains of events recorded in *The South African Baptist*. Healed, he returned to his church and his beloved people, not the same Duma.

## Chapter 15

# William Duma and His Boys

Rev. Clifford Nxumalo was in his teens when he first got to know the Pastor. He recalled, 'He had a personality which magnetised the young. He was always surrounded by a group of youths and young men. His life of transparent holiness fascinated them, his teaching disturbed them, his humour delighted them.'

For Clifford a facet of the Pastor's ministry which was of tremendous importance was his 'shepherding'. He explained, 'I have been learning from him for a very long time. When as boys we attended his church, some of us living in his home were put under strict training. Nowhere else have I found such a good preparation for those who sought to be God's ambassadors. When he noticed youths or young men about the home or church he would call them and say, "I want to see you, and you, this evening" (usually six or seven of us). On our arrival he would make no comment. We sat and waited while he went about his affairs ... wondering. Eventually, usually about 10.00 p.m., he would call us to his office with our Bibles. He would explain that he had delayed until the rest of the household were in bed because he didn't want any interruptions. "Do you have any problems?" he would ask, and we would relate the problems and difficulties about which we needed the Lord's help.

'Pastor Duma emphasised, "You can't pray for the Kingdom if you are heavily laden and you have not told the Lord about your need. You must unstrap your burden, lay aside your weight and get rid of your personal affairs. Only then can you intercede for the church of God, its needs and the wider needs of the nation. And those are the things you must learn to handle before God."

'When all our needs had been dealt with in prayer, he read scriptures. I noticed that he was well acquainted with the strong man in Mark 3:27: *"In fact, no one can enter a strong man's house and carry off his possessions, unless he first ties up the strong man. Then he can rob his house."* He expounded, "The first thing you do before you can get power over a strong man is to tie him up. You see by this why I have called you to prayer while others sleep. This strong man is only tied up by prayer. We are going to pray until the morning." If you were tired or sleepy, you just had to shake yourself up.

'He encouraged us to pray one by one, urging us to take our time. "You must know what you are praying about." When each of us had prayed, he took over. When that big teacher on prayer began to pray, we would feel as though we had not prayed at all! It seemed as if somewhere, somehow, we had missed the high water mark of his soaring intercessions, and so we had. When he prayed, the big guns blazed and lifted us right up and up. That was what we always waited for – a sense of the heavens coming down. Those sessions continued until 3.00 or 4.00 a.m. We had been through the mangle of the Holy Spirit's power.

'After all that, in those early morning hours he would ask, "Do you wish to sleep?"

' "If we go to sleep, we'll never get up in time for work."

' "Don't worry, I'll waken you." He put us on the floor in the dining room, saying, "You can lie there. You are warriors of prayer – you don't need comforting with beds. I'll cover you with blankets."

'When he wakened us at 5.00 a.m. with flowers in his hand, having already returned from market, we wondered when he had slept. When younger, he had little time for sleep. We observed that when he arose from prayer, he was not so much like a soldier clothed in steel against the enemy, but like the eagle that soars in the upper air and does not worry about how it is to cross the river.'

Clifford recalled an occasion in the 1950s when Pastor Duma, having returned recently from fasting for twenty-one days, said, 'Clifford, I want you to come with me to visit a church member.' The tin town, fourteen miles from Durban, was called Ten and Three.

'Alighting from a bus, we commenced the long walk to the home. As we walked, two black men were approaching us. As they drew near it sounded as if one of them was grumbling to himself in a loud voice. I concluded he was drunk or mental. As we were about to pass them, he suddenly jumped like a buck, shouting, "There is a minister! Hau! That's bad luck for me!" I was shaken. Neither of us wore clerical garb. Then in a wild raging voice, he howled, "Don't torment us."

'I was very annoyed. I asked Pastor if he knew the man. How did he guess we were of the church?'

' "I don't know him."

' "Then why did you keep quiet when he shouted at you like that?"

' "Clifford, young man, you've got a lot to learn."

' "What?"

'He replied, "That man is demon possessed. Why do you imagine he cried, 'Don't torment us?' "

'So I learned something! Pastor continued, "My boy, you must learn that when a demon shouts at you, your biggest weapon is silence. Don't answer back. By keeping quiet you have knocked the demon down." That was my first lesson in demon possession.'

Pastor Clifford went on to learn much more from the Pastor on the subject of demon deliverance, in particular how to distinguish between those who have demonic spirits and those with physical ailments. Duma was able to determine from the sufferers' reactions whether or not they were demon possessed. He explained, 'The Prayer

Circle assistants put each suspected case in front of me. I endeavour to get him to look straight at me – I just stand doing nothing. If he dodges my look I continue looking at him in a patient, normal kindly way. Almost always there are desperate efforts to avoid my eyes. If the victim succeeds, I grip him and at that instant he falls down.'

Pastor Clifford enjoyed telling the story of Skonyena. 'We had knowledge of Skonyena for a long time but didn't know he was demon possessed. His aunt attended Umgeni Road and one Wednesday brought Skonyena with her. Short and slightly built, he had to be tied with rope because of his cunning and violence. He was left under close observation in the vestry. We were assured that Pastor was safe from attack. Entering the vestry, Duma went right up to him. Skonyena was in a rage, roaring loud and long with gruff, throaty, animal sounds. Pastor ordered the removal of the ropes. Released, he retreated and dodged as Pastor advanced toward him. I now understand that the demon in him, like those of Gadara, feared exorcism. Unable to attract and hold his eyes, Pastor put his hands on him. Suddenly Pastor was lifted high by Skonyena's right arm, so that his feet were in the air. Horrified, we rushed to his assistance. As Pastor touched the ground he faced him. They stood face to face. With a frighteningly loud voice, as if amplified by many microphones, Duma addressed the demon, "Get out!" While Pastor invoked the power of Almighty God, the demon left him. The man slowly crumpled and fell to the ground, but "Baba" has never been allowed to forget his trapeze act!'

One of Clifford's most vivid memories of Pastor Duma took place one Prayer Circle morning at Umgeni Road. 'An African woman with a baby on her back crept into the church. Pastor noticed that she was carrying a heavy basket and despatched me to help her. She was from Pondoland and had travelled many miles seeking relief for her child's appalling condition. Finally she made for McCord's Zulu

Mission Hospital in Durban. There, once again, her hope was crushed. She was told, "We can do nothing."

'All hope gone, forlorn and weeping, she sat on a veranda with the babe on her back. Nxele, one of Duma's young men, then a clerk at the hospital, noticed her and asked her what was wrong. She repeated her story of heartbreak. Sitting down beside her, he slowly explained to her confused mind that he knew of only one who could help her – a man of prayer. Patiently he explained how to find the church.

'When I took her basket and saw the child's head, enormously swollen, my heart turned a somersault, my faith blurred and went out. The child was suffering from hydrocephalus. Pastor instructed me to take the mother to the vestry as the sight of the malformed child would distract the worshippers. Their eyes would certainly not close in prayer!

'The child's wide staring eyes, never closed. Wherever I looked I seemed to see them. I couldn't bear the woman's sorrow. I left the vestry, went into the church and told Pastor, "The woman weeps and weeps. Tears stream down her cheeks like water from a broken tap. She doesn't seem to have eaten either."

'I knew of Pastor's tremendous compassion. He went to the vestry and, seeing her sorrow, told me to take her into church. Then he did something unthinkable! He turned his back on the packed church, leaving them to pray or stare and gave his entire attention to the case.

'Very lightly with one deft finger he touched the top of the child's head. "Clifford," he commanded – and I knew by his voice the Divine Authority was upon him – "run to the house, pour water into the special white basin I use and get my prayer cloth."

'I rushed to the house, wondering what it was all about. I felt confused. Through the years I had never seen Pastor do such a thing as to leave worshippers and those waiting for healing prayer. On my return with the basin, he told me to put it on the floor. He took the prayer cloth. By this time the congregation was a picture of amazed, questioning faces just staring.

'Quietly he said to me, "Bring the child and mother. You hold the child." I looked at him, horrified. He repeated, "Hold the child up."

'He dipped the cloth in cold water, squeezed water from it and gently he placed the wet cloth on the child's head. I stared to see, before long, a thin stream of steam rising from the head. He repeated the process, then as I continued holding the child, he laid on hands proclaiming, "In the Name of Jesus of Nazareth." Then I saw his hands shake with a great trembling and I knew the Holy Spirit was upon him. He repeated, "In the Name of Jesus, Oh Doctor Jesus." An intense silence gripped the people. Then in a low, quiet voice he said, "I know the Lord has done the work." A short prayer. "It is all right, little mother." To me, "Take them to the vestry, tell them to return home, all will be well."

'In the vestry I slowly explained the meaning of the ceremony. She took it lightly as if she were eager to talk of something else. To my astonishment she began, "When I entered the church I heard someone saying, '*Mfundisi* is in need of a car.' I feel we need this man. Take this two shillings to help."

' "Mama, our *Umfundisi* will never take your money. He is a very sympathetic man, he wouldn't allow it." Then I became a messenger running between *Umfundisi* and the woman, all about two shillings. I said "Baba, the woman is so touched she sends two shillings towards your car."

' "Tell her she must keep it to buy food."

'She insisted I take it back to him. Finally she left it on the table.

'For six months we heard nothing. One day a very soiled envelope arrived. Pastor said, "I can't read the writing. You read it to me."

' "Whoever this is," I said, "is not a Zulu. The spellings differ, it comes from a Pondo." It began, "*Mfundisi*, you will remember a Pondo woman with a child who had a very large head. I returned to my kraal. All the way I wondered what would happen. Let me tell you quickly that the child now has a normal head, only a very, very tiny lump remains which shrinks daily. She is walking, she sleeps well, she will soon be quite normal." This was a great moment for Pastor – and for me also. I had held the baby!'

## Chapter 16

# No Other Name

Sufferers from all walks of life and all shades of colour visited Umgeni Road. They arrived with all the torments life can impose. Having visited psychiatrists, psychologists, medical practitioners, witchdoctors, when brave hope was dying in the heart, they heard of a Zulu and found their way to his humble door. By plane, car, train, sometimes by long-distance telephone, or by cable, sufferers sought the man of prayer. In his presence they found themselves pouring out their miseries with strange abandon. Endowed with a profound compassion, Duma would sit back, as if he had all the time in the world in which to listen. Looking at him they could see in his quiet eyes, deep pools of undisturbed serenity and peace.

It has been suggested that the 'pull' of his ministry was his power in prayer for healing. Duma would quickly refute that suggestion. 'Never,' he said, 'do I pray for healing without probing into the sufferer's spiritual condition. The insatiable hunger of my heart in all I do is to help bring about a love pact between God and the sufferer.'

Duma was a man of certainty who would not deviate from waiting on God for His leading. In Johannesburg, 1976, while he was ministering in a white church for ten days, he was approached by another church to return to minister among them at a later date. 'We urgently need you. We have difficulties.' Showing him the dates they said,

'Choose your own dates. Even though we have planned, we will alter anything if you will come.'

He replied, 'You know I do not promise anything until I receive God's green light.'

'But you could mark a date for when you get the green light.'

'Oh no! If I come, it will be on God's date, not on any date you or I have chosen.'

The gift of discernment operated within Duma with a disconcerting and sometimes embarrassing effectiveness. When he was conducting a service, suddenly in the pulpit he would suffer an acute pain which alerted him to the fact that someone in the building was suffering from a disease in the same organ. Often it was the heart. He would be compelled through his own temporary indisposition to interrupt the service, describe his condition and ask a sufferer with similar symptoms to stand up. Quite often several would stand. He would search each face until he saw the one whom he knew without any doubt was the sufferer. He would request that he or she came forward, or, if unable to, that the individual be carried forward. Duma would then leave the pulpit, often with difficulty. As soon as he lay hands on the patient, his own pain instantly ceased and the sufferer usually was suddenly free. The variety of diseases he was enabled to identify under divine revelation was amazing.

When healing during the Wednesday morning service, Duma would stand on a slightly raised platform, with the inner circle standing around him in silent prayer. The sick were brought, one by one and prayed for individually. Sometimes he anointed them with oil, or laid on hands; at other times he called others to lay on hands, but quite often something unplanned was done under the strong compulsion of the Holy Spirit. If the ill required support, they were helped or carried forward. A qualified sister of long experience was always at hand.

Duma explained: 'Leaving my prayer chamber for the Prayer Circle, I do not allow anyone to shake hands with me. I have discovered that shaking hands with people has noticeably depleted the power given me. I feel it at once.

'If, on the morning of the healing service, I find that, for various reasons, I'm not standing immovably as a rock on the promise of God for His power, I cancel prayers for healing and conduct a "heart-searching for God, a thirsting for His living water". I tell the people candidly that they would not want me to deceive them by praying in the flesh when I know the power is not resident within me in the totality I experience on other occasions. They would resent a doctor misleading them, still more a servant of God because he was too proud to acknowledge the temporary absence of that power. Too many Christian healers have fallen by the wayside after a period of exciting success because they have given way to pride. For me, *"I resolved to know nothing while I was with you except Jesus Christ and him crucified."*

In order to avoid falling into the pit of self-congratulation Duma read very few of the hundreds of glowing letters he received through the years. They were filed away by a selected worker.

A frequent discussion among Christian and other observers of healing services centres around the phenomenon of sufferers falling to the ground when a healer lays his or her hands on them in prayer. Duma was emphatic that falling is not a sign of a person, seeking to be fully surrendered to God, being filled with the Holy Spirit. In his view it was often a sign that all in the deep and secret places of a person was not surrendered to God – a sign of a battle between the Holy Spirit and Satan.

In other cases it is demon possession that occasions the resistance and falling. As the evil spirit within a victim battles to resist exorcism, frequently the possessed falls to the ground and sometimes is thrown violently about.

Wednesday mornings sometimes had their disturbing moments. One such occasion was a morning in March 1976 when the atmosphere was full of expectancy and the sick were there in great numbers. Before the queue was reduced by half, an intruder insisted on being taken to the Pastor at once. To avoid the possibility of others being distracted he was led directly to Duma. With his keen discernment, the Pastor challenged the man, 'Are you a believer in Jesus Christ?'

'No, I am not, I am a Hindu and satisfied with my religion.'

Duma handed the middle-aged Indian to a counsellor saying, 'I have a long queue waiting, I can't waste time.'

He was returned to Duma with the comment, 'He wants nothing to do with Jesus Christ. He wants only prayer for healing.'

Facing him for a moment in silence, Duma said, 'Dear man, how am I going to pray for you without Christ? You know I am a Christian. I pray in and through the Name of the Redeemer and Saviour, Jesus Christ our Lord, but you reject Him. How then, in what Name, to what Name, am I to pray? He is the only spiritual Doctor I seek to heal the sick. All have heard me countless times address our Lord, the Almighty One, as "Doctor Jesus". Dear man, I have no other Name but Jesus. You refuse it. My heart is sad for you. I can't help you. You will have to leave with all your sickness. Jesus Christ is not a beggar on the road waiting to be used by anyone for anything. He is King of Kings and Lord of Lords. He said, *"If you ask anything in my name I will do it"'* (John 14:14).

Turning to the congregation Duma said, 'Let me warn you who bring friends here, not to invite the sick without ascertaining if they are believers in Jesus Christ or not. I do not want such to be turned away disappointed.' With his hand on the man's shoulder Duma said, 'It grieves me deeply that you have to go empty away, but I know of no other Name.'

The man, his face distorted with hate, left to go 'to his own place'. He died shortly afterwards.

On another occasion a man arrived just as the service was starting. Pastor confronted him with the question, 'Are you a Christian?'

'No, but we Hindus also pray for the sick.'

'Why, if your temple prays for the sick, do you come here?'

'I thought I would come here. I am a businessman. Do me a favour.'

Duma related, 'With brazen effrontery he fumbled with the inner pocket of his coat, took out an envelope and showed me a cheque. I said, "Wait a minute." I called counsellor Rev. Francis of St Aidan's Indian Church to deal with him. I reported that the man had come like a devil to buy God off. To the would-be buyer I said, "I may be poor, I may eat simply, but if I were dressed in sacking I would never do what you request."

'He was an educated man. Father Francis spoke in English and as I listened I was fully satisfied. Father said, "I am a Priest of a Parish. I came here with my ill wife. She was healed. This man cannot be bought with money."

Haughtily he walked away with his tarnished money. I thought of thirty pieces of silver.'

✣ ✣ ✣

Beauty Dhlamini had been carried into the vestry of the church by her relatives at 8.00 a.m. There she lay, waiting for the intercessory service which commenced at 11.00 a.m. Once a nursing sister, she had been as beautiful as her name. Now in her early thirties and in the grip of cancer only a hint of former loveliness remained. A biopsy had established the diagnosis of 'incurable'. She was discharged from hospital to be with her family.

Sister Magwaza, one of the counsellors who had herself been dramatically healed with only three months to live, confessed that on seeing Beauty she thought, 'This woman is not only a terminal case, but I doubt if she will survive the day. Is it any use for Pastor to pray for her?' Suddenly deeply ashamed of her doubts she recovered her faith and helped the relatives to carry Beauty to the healing line, where she was slowly lowered into a much cushioned chair to receive the Pastor's first prayer.

He explained to the full congregation that, although Mrs Dhlamini had been waiting since 8.00 a.m., he could not pray for her in private because her case was for the great glory of God and could not be hidden in a back room. He had, in special prayer, received the assurance that she would be healed. The 'assurance' he referred to was no easy word lightly spoken. It was the result of years of intercession, during which he had become familiar with the goodness of the Lord in assuring him of the miracle before the prayer. It was the same most holy intimacy Jesus Himself knew before the miracle of Lazarus when He said, *'Father, I thank You that You have heard Me'* (John 11:41).

Approaching Beauty, Pastor encouraged her to have faith. He anointed her with oil and she was carried to the vestry where Sister Magwaza described the scene.

'Not long after Pastor's prayer she was in agonising pain in the lower abdominal region. She sweated and tossed as her tears trickled down her face. I myself cried to see her. I told her it was a common occurrence after Pastor's prayer for the pain to worsen till it reached its peak when relief and healing came. Pastor and Mrs Duma came to the vestry.

'Pastor knelt by her side and, under compulsion, involuntarily began to massage the abdomen. As we watched, we noticed relief stealing over her face, then he prayed a second time. I stood astounded. I had never heard him pray with such intimacy and persuasion through all the years I had worked with him. It was like a conversation between Jesus and himself, or again like a baby begging his Father and then, gaining courage, he began demanding. I was shocked. He had always taught us we could not, may not, demand anything of God. Then I thought, "God must be leading him in a different way this time." As I listened, he said, "I'm your servant, you are using me now and again, but Father, today, do the special thing here and do it now; not in three weeks, not two weeks, not even in a few hours, but now, I plead, oh my Father, in Jesus' Name, now, please."

'Pastor later described his interior experience when interceding: "I entered a dark cloud, bleak and lonely as midnight. Baffled, I tunnelled my way on and on and on, unconscious of anything anywhere. I battled determinedly along until I knew for certain I was through. It was victory." '

Beauty lay in the vestry and on her face was peace. Duma called Mrs Magwaza to run to the shop for an egg and meet him at his house near the vestry.

She said, 'I ran, all right, wondering what on earth the egg was for. I decided that the Lord was now using him in a different way.'

She found him warming milk for an egg flip which they took to Beauty, who was smiling, her pain gone. The egg flip, apart from a little nourishment, seemed to have no significance apart from the fact, very important to Duma, that he had obeyed a strong leading. He prayed with her a third time, after which, of her own volition, she arose and walked through the church to the waiting car.

At the intercessory service the following week the church was silent as Pastor recounted the story of Beauty. All eyes focused intently on their Baba. Suddenly he stopped. They waited, wondering, until he cried, 'There she is.' The whole church turned to look. Beauty, her weight slightly increased, her face, its beauty returning, was scarcely recognisable. Eagerly, she told her wonderful story and gave thanks to God. Her husband, with shining face, was there to give himself publicly to God. The church was vibrant with the glory of it all.

# Chapter 17

# A Man for All Seasons,
# A Man for All Places,
# A Man for All Races

It was a momentous occasion in the Swazi nation's history. In May 1973 the Prime Minister for the government of King Sobhuza II, Prince M. Dhalamini, was preparing his presentation in parliament of a new Royal Constitution for the Swazi people, and there was a clear danger that this could precipitate a national crisis.

An added anxiety was the ill health of the Prime Minister who was suffering from the effects of a stroke which obstructed the free movement of an arm and affected his speech. He was deeply troubled. How could he adequately present the all-important Royal Constitution with a slurred diction? It was not surprising at such a time, in such a disturbed world, that the nation's leaders were apprehensive and that their hearts were full of fear.

Mr Manzini MP, a strong believer in prayer who had been converted under Duma's ministry, urged the Prime Minister to ask Pastor Duma to come for the purpose of prayer. And so, on the night before the Constitution was to be presented, a car hastened to Swaziland with Pastor Duma accompanied by the Rev. J.F. Francis, Rector of St Aidan's Anglican Church, and Mr Hoffman and Mr McKenzie. At the border government cars were waiting to transport them to the home of the Prime Minister. Anointed by the power of the Holy Spirit, Duma made the simple, urgent request that the speech impediment and paralysed arm would be healed, that Prince Dhalamini might have freedom of spirit and freedom of speech, and that the new Royal Constitution might have a totally peaceful reception with neither disturbances nor opposition. During his prayer, he received a divine assurance that by the next day the Prime Minister would be a transformed man, his arm free, and his speech normal.

The following morning, King Sobhuza II, Knight of the British Empire, requested Pastor Duma and his group to go to the palace to pray that there might be no unrest, nor public opposition during the presentation of the new constitution. He also requested prayer for himself, as he was also unwell.

The Servant of God, with a warm smile, gentle voice and holy dignity, answered the King's request, saying, 'I can pray for the peaceful introduction and reception of the new Constitution, I can pray for your health because you need prayer personally, but I can't pray for you as the King. You are the King of Swaziland, but you must first bow down to my King, King Jesus.'

The King replied, 'I have heard many things in my life, but as far as I am concerned it seemed to me that this Christ was dead. Now, He has come alive through this man speaking to me in such a manner.' The King then knelt, confessed his belief in Jesus Christ and admitted that Jesus was King of Kings. Pastor then said, 'Now I can pray for you.'

As the group was leaving, the King repeatedly said, 'This is a moment in my life I will never forget. I don't know why you didn't let me know about this *Umfundisi* who has brought God to the palace.'

From the palace they were taken to the Parliament. The Constitution was introduced in complete silence with no opposition and was passed without any objections. That same day, King Sobhuza, although long past seventy and not well, spoke in the open air to over 7,000 of his people, one hundred per cent of whom accepted the Constitution without a breath of trouble.

✦ ✦ ✦

Towards the end of 1976 William Duma suffered a heart attack. When able to leave McCord's Hospital he went to the home of one of his 'bird cage' men, Evangelist Nxele, in Zululand, to be nursed back to health by Mrs Nxele, a trained nurse. Early in 1977 his old friend Mr Manzini took him to his home in Swaziland for a month to recuperate.

He returned to Durban with a permanent fever – not of the body but of the spirit – a fever which was a passion to win souls for Christ. From his pulpit in Umgeni Road he told his people, 'I am eaten up with the burning desire to win souls. My people, I want to see you all in heaven.'

As time passed, the 'fever' did not diminish. As if wanting to make the most of his remaining time, during three consecutive extremely hot days, he elected to visit three different towns, each some distance from Durban. He travelled in a car through the heat, held a service and returned home to sleep. His friends dreaded another collapse. Impervious to their concern, he toiled, planned and consumed his energies as if he knew instinctively that his days were numbered.

He journeyed to Zululand where he baptised thirteen. Then, on 21 August, another twenty-eight were baptised at Umgeni Road.

Then, to the surprise of his people, he announced that on Wednesday 5 October a special baptismal service would be substituted for the normal Prayer Circle meeting. Never before had he departed from the normal practice of his ministry and his congregation felt a secret aching premonition. They noticed that he took such an unusual interest in the personal arrangement of that service. Why Wednesday and not Sunday?

He also urgently invited people who normally did not attend the Wednesday service to make a special effort to be there. He even included those whom he knew were

working. All he was doing was contrary to his normal
pastoral custom. Mrs Freeman was specially asked to be
present to sing one of his favourite solos.

One of the church members, Mrs Maria Ngubane, who
was converted under the Pastor's ministry, recalled the
service. 'On that morning, Wednesday 5 October, 1977,
the church was full to capacity. Pastor Duma, wearing a
white gown, led the service. As I looked at him, his face
shone like an angel. After the opening hymn and prayer
he called for the soloist, Mrs Freeman, whom he had
specially invited to sing. However, before she sang, he spoke
strangely to the congregation. They were amazed, shocked.
He said, "I have asked Mrs Freeman to sing at this service
because when I was away ill, I knew that I was going home
to Jesus. I have asked her to sing today the hymn which she
will sing at my funeral service." He continued, "Even today,
I am not afraid of death because I am going to see my
Jesus."

'The whole congregation was deeply affected. Before
singing, Mrs Freeman said, "I am thankful, Pastor Duma,
because I am no longer going to sing at your funeral, because
Jesus has healed you, but I will come again to sing while you
are alive!" As she sang, the sanctuary was filled with the
presence of Jesus. All over the church, people were wiping
tears away.

'Pastor Duma thanked her and repeated the amazing
statement saying, "Thank you, Mrs Freeman, that you will
come again to sing whilst I am still living. But you might
not, because I am longing to see my Jesus soon and to be
with Him always." The joy of the Lord was on his face as he
spoke.

'The evangelist, Pastor Elijah Maswangani from Tzaneen,
Transvaal, was guest speaker. He spoke on Colossians 2:5–7,
as a man giving counsel to the church whose Pastor had just
gone to the glory land. We thought it amazing because
Pastor Duma was very much alive and listening himself.

'Four believers were to be baptised, a white couple from
Cape Town and an Indian couple. When Pastor was about

to baptise the Indian woman, he asked for her confession of Jesus. His face suddenly looked grey and strange. The words he spoke were blurred and could not be clearly understood. I thought the Lord was baptising him afresh in the Holy Spirit as Christ's Presence was so deeply felt throughout the church. However, he recovered miraculously and completed the service. He left the water as if nothing had gone wrong with him.'

The service over, Duma invited the visitors to the manse for refreshments, after which he went to rest. Disturbed about his condition, someone went to see how he was. He found him very restless, obviously in pain, but attempting to hide it. That night he was in a serious condition in McCord's Hospital, the hospital in which, for many years, he had taken regular services for the nurses. From Wednesday night to Saturday he lay very ill. On Saturday 8 October 1977 he died.

The funeral service, held a week later at the Central Baptist Church, Durban, was packed to more than capacity. All over the building three people were sitting on two chairs, aisles were filled and the entrance was crowded with people standing. The outside pavements and the street were full of mourners. The four races of the Republic and leaders of several denominations were there. All wanted to say thank-you for the life of Pastor William Duma, to glorify God for the life of such a man – a man for all seasons.

*Brief Tribute by the President on behalf of the Baptist Union and the SA Baptist Missionary Society at the Funeral of William Duma on Saturday 15 October, 1977:*

We have come to honour a man of God for all seasons, one whose outstanding devotion to his Lord and whose service for his fellow men did not vary with the wind and the weather. He was the same yesterday and today because his walk was close with the One who is the same forever.

We have come from every part of our fair land to honour a man of God for all places. By air, land and sea, he travelled within our country and beyond its borders answering a series of Macedonian calls for spiritual help and healing.

We have come together to honour a man of God for all races. When William Duma was praying, all the lines of division disappeared and we were bound together in a fellowship of love.

We have come together to honour a man of God for all cases. If everyone here were to write down cases known to us – where our Lord's healing touch has been graciously given through the ministry of our brother, it would make thrilling reading.

It was our great privilege at the Rosebank Union Church to have Pastor Duma for the last evangelical mission which he conducted. My wife and I were privileged to have Pastor and his assistant Pastor Clifford Nxumalo, staying in our home for the period of that mission, a mission singularly owned and used of God. With close contact in mind, together with a period of thirty years of intermittent fellowship, I can honestly say that I thank my God upon every remembrance of him (Philippians 1:3).

There are not many of God's servants of whom such a claim can be made – 'every remembrance' a cause for thanksgiving – every remembrance made a sweet savour of Christ his Lord, whom he loved and served in all seasons, all places, ministering to all cases among all races. Thanks be to God for every remembrance of him.

## Key to Zulu words used in the text

| | |
|---|---|
| *Amasi* | sour milk |
| *Baba* | father |
| *Doek* | headdress |
| *Elangeni* | in the sun |
| *Ibhokisi* | box, coffin |
| *Indaba* | discussion |
| *Inyanga* | herbalist |
| *Izinyanga* | medicine men |
| *Mfundisi* | minister, teacher |
| *Mnumzane* | master |
| *Nomvula* | 'with the rain' |
| *Talani* | thank you |
| *Ukhamba* | clay pot |
| *Umfana* | boy |
| *Umfundisi* | minister |
| *Umvelinqangi* | lit. 'One who appeared before all' |
| *Umthakathi* | those who have devilish power of bewitchment |
| *Unkulunkulu* | the Great One (God) |

If you have enjoyed this book and would like to help us to send a copy of it and many other titles to needy pastors in the **Third World**, please write for further information or send your gift to:

**Sovereign World Trust**
**PO Box 777, Tonbridge**
**Kent TN11 0ZS**
**United Kingdom**

or to the **'Sovereign World'** distributor in your country.

Visit our website at **www.sovereign-world.org**
for a full range of Sovereign World books.